Cicero's Orations
Against
Catiline

Literal Translation

by
Rev. Dr. Giles

This facsimile reproduction of a rare out of print work is presented as a service. There may be places where the text is indistinct.

Contents

CICERO'S ORATIONS

AGAINST CATALINE.

Oration 1.

Quousque how long *tandem* at length, *Catilina* Cataline, *abutere* will you abuse *patientia nostra* our patience? *Quamdiu* how long *etiam* also *furor iste tuus* will that phrenzy of yours *eludet nos* mock at us ? *Quem ad finem* to what limit *effrenata audacia* will your unrestrained audacity *jactabit sese* boast itself? *Nocturnumne præsidium* has the nightly garrison *Palatii* of the Palatium *te* [moved] thee *nihil* not at all, *vigiliæ* the watches *urbis* of the city *nihil* not at all, *timor* the fear *populi* of the people *nihil* not at all, *concursus* the meetings *omnium bonorum* of all good men *nihil* not at all, *hic munitissimus locus* this entrenched place *habendi senatus* of holding the senate, *ora* have the looks *vultusque* and countenances *horum* of these men here *moverunt* moved you *nihil* not at all ? *Non sentis* do you not feel *tua consilia* that your plans *patere* are laid open? *Non vides* do you not see *conjurationem tuam* that your conspiracy *jam teneri* is already held *constrictam* bound *conscientia* by the common knowledge *omnium horum* of all these [senators]? *Quid* what *egeris* you did *proxima nocte* last night, *quid* what *superiore* the night before, *ubi* where *fueris* you were, *quos* what men *convocaveris* you called together, *quid consilii* what counsel *ceperis*

1

you took, *quem* which *nostrum* of us *arbitraris* do you think *ignorare* is ignorant? 2. *O tempora* oh for these times! *O mores* oh for our morals! *Senatus* the senate *intelligit* knows *hæc* these facts: *consul* the consul *videt* sees them; *hic tamen* yet this man *vivit* lives. *Vivit* lives? *immo vero* nay indeed *etiam venit* he even comes *in senatum* into the senate; *fit* he is made *particeps* a participator *publici consilii* of the public counsels; *notat* he marks *et designat* and points out *oculis* with his eyes *ad cædem* for slaughter *unumquemque* every one *nostrum* of us. *Nos autem* but we, *viri fortes* brave men, *videmur* seem *satisfacere* to do enough *reipublicæ* for the state, *si* if *vitemus* we avoid *furorem* the madness *ac tela* and weapons *istius* of that man. *Oportebat* it was right *te* that you, *Catilina* Catiline, *jampridem* long ago *duci* should be dragged *ad mortem* to death *jussu* by command *consulis* of the consul: *pestem istam* that the destruction, *quam* which *tu* you *jamdiu machinaris* have now long been contriving *in nos omnes* for all of us, *conferri* should be heaped *in te* upon yourself. *An vero* did indeed *vir amplissimus* that most excellent man *Publius Scipio* Publius Scipio, *pontifex maximus* the supreme pontiff, *privatus* though a private man, *interfecit* slay *Tiberium Gracchum* Tiberius Gracchus *labefactantem* who was shaking *statum* the condition *reipublicæ* of the republic *mediocriter* slightly, *nos vero* but shall we *consules* consuls *perferemus* put up with *Catilinam* Catiline *cupientum* who is desiring *vastare* to lay waste *orbem* the globe *terræ* of the earth *cæde* with slaughter *atque incendiis* and conflagration? *Nam* for *prætereo* I pass over *illa* those things *nimis antiqua* too ancient, *quod* how that *Caius Servilius Ahala* Caius Servilius Ahala *occidit* slew *sua manu* with his own hand *Spurium Mælium* Spurius Mælius *studentem* who was labouring *novis rebus* for a revolution. *Fuit* there was, *quondam* formerly *ista virtus* such virtue *in hac republica* in this republic, *ut* that *viri fortes* brave men *coercerent* coerced *civem*

2

perniciosum a dangerous citizen *acrioribus suppliciis* with severer punishment *quam* than *acerbissimum hostem* the bitterest enemy. *Habemus* we have *in te* against you, *Catilina* Catiline, *senatusconsultum* a decree of the senate *vehemens* strong *et grave* and severe : *non deest* there is not wanting *reipublicæ* to the republic *consilium* counsel *neque* nor *auctoritas* the influence *hujus ordinis* of this order ; *nos* we, *dico* I say it *aperte* openly, *nos* we *consules* consuls *desumus* are wanting.

II. 4. *Senatus* the senate *quondam* formerly *decrevit* decreed, *ut* that *Lucius Opimius* Lucius Opimius *consul* the consul *videret* should look to it *ne* lest *respublica* the republic *caperet* should receive *quid detrimenti* any damage. *Nox nulla* not a single night *intercessit* intervened, *Caius Gracchus* Caius Gracchus *natus* born *clarissimo patre* of a most noble father, *avo* grandfather, *majoribus* and ancestors, *interfectus est* was slain *propter* on account of *quasdam suspiciones* certain suspicions *seditionum* of seditions : *Marcus Fulvius* Marcus Fulvius *consularis* a man of consular rank, *occisus est* was slain *cum liberis* with his children. *Simili senatusconsulto* by a similiar decree of the senate *respublica* the republic *permissa est* was committed *consulibus* to the consuls *Caio Mario* Caius Marius *et* and *Lucio Valerio* Lucius Valerius : *num mors* did death *ac pœna* and punishment *populi Romani* of [from] the Roman people *unum diem* for a single day *postea* after that *remorata est* delay *Lucium Saturninum* Lucius Saturninus *tribunum* tribune *plebis* of the people *et* and *Caium Servilium* Caius Servilius *prætorem* the prætor? *At nos* but we *jam* now *vicesimum diem* for the twentieth day *patimur* are suffering *aciem* the edge *auctoritatis* of the authority *horum* of these [senators] *hebescere* to be blunted. *Habemus enim* for we have *senatusconsultum* a decree of the senate *hujusmodi* of this kind, *veruntamen* but however *inclusum* inclosed *in tabulis* in the papers, *tanquam* as *gladium* a sword *reconditum* buried *in vagina* in the scabbard : *quo ex senatusconsulto* by which decree of the senate *convenit* it is fit, *Catilina* Catiline, *te* that you *esse interfectum* should be slain *confestim* at once. *Vivis* you live! *et vivis* and you live *non* not *ad deponendam* to lay aside, *sed* but *ad confirmandam audaciam* to confirm your audacity. *Cupio* I desire, *patres conscripti* conscript fathers, *me* that I *esse clementem* may be merciful : *cupio* I desire, *in tantis periculis* amid such great dangers *reipublicæ* of the republic, *me* that I *non videri* may not seem *dissolutum* negligent : *sed* but *jam* already *ipse* I myself *condemno me* condemn myself *inertiæ* of sloth *nequitiæque* and of remissness. 5. *Castra sunt* there is a camp *collocata* placed *in Italia* in Italy *in faucibus* in the gorges *Etruriæ* of Etruria *contra rempublicam* in hostility to the republic : *numerus* the number *hostium* of the enemies *crescit* grows *in dies singulos* every day, *videmus autem* but we see *imperatorem* the commander-in-chief *eorum castrorum* of that camp *ducemque* and the leader *hostium* of the enemies *intra mœnia* within the walls *atque adeo* and even *iu senatu* in the senate, *quotidie* daily *molientem* designing *perniciem aliquam intestinam* some intestine destruction *reipublicæ* against the state. *Si* if *jussero* I shall command *te* you, *Catilina* Catiline, *jam* now *comprehendi* to be seized, *si* if *interfici* to be put to death, *erit mihi verendum* I shall have to fear *ne non* that *omnes boni* all good men [may say] *hoc* that this *esse factum* has been done *a me* by me *serius* too late *potius* rather *quam* than *quisquam* that any one *dicat* may say [that it has been done] *crudelius* too cruelly. *Verum* but *ego* I *certa de causa* for a certain reason *nondum adducor* am not yet led *ut faciam* to do *hoc* this *quod* which *oportuit factum esse* ought to have been done *jampridem* long ago. *Tum* then *denique* at last *interficiam te* I shall put you to death *quum* when *jam* already *nemo* no one *poterit* will be able *inveniri* to be found *tam improbus* so wicked, *tam perditus* so abandoned *tam similis* so like *tui* yourself, *qui non fateatur* as not to confess *id* that it *factum esse* was done *jure* justly. 6. *Quamdiu* as long *is erit* there shall **be** *quisquam* any one *qui* who *auleat* dares *defendere te* to defend you, *vives* you will live ; *et* and *vives* you will live *ita* so *ut* as *vivis* you live *nunc* now, *obsessus* beleaguered *meis multis* by my many *et firmis præsidiis* and strong guards, *ne possis* that you may not be able *commovere te* to stir yourself *contra rempublicam* against the republic: *etiam* also *oculi* the eyes *et aures* and the ears *multorum* of many *speculabuntur* will spy out *atque custodient* and guard *te* you, *sunt* as *adhuc fecerunt* they have hitherto done, *r on sentientem* though you do not perceive it.

III. *Etenim* for too *quid est* what is there, *Catilina* Catiline, *quo d* which *jam* now *expecies* you can expect *amplius* any longer, *si* if *neque nox* neither the night *potest* can *obscurare* hide *cœtus nefarios* your wicked meetings *tenebris* in darkness, *nec* nor *privata domus* a private house *continere* contain *parietibus* within its walls *vocem* the voice *conjurationis tuæ* of your conspiracy? *si* if *omnia* all things *illustrantur* are brought to light, *si* if *erumpunt* they break forth? *Muta jam* change at once *istam mentem* that mind of yours; *crede mihi* trust me ; *obliviscere* forget *cædis* slaughter *atque incendiorum* and flames. *Teneris* you are hemmed in *undique* on every side; *omnia tua consilia* all your plans *sunt* are *clariora* more clear *luce* than the light *nobis* to us: *quæ* which [plans] *etiam* also *licet recognoscas* you may pass in review *mecum* with me.
7. *Meministine* do you remember *me* that I *dicere* said *in senatu* in the senate *ante diem duodecimum* on the twelfth day before *Calendas Novembres* the calends of November, *Caium Manlium* that Caius Manlius *satellitem* the satellite *atque administrum* and minister *tuæ audaciæ* of your audacity, *fore* would be *in armis* in arms *certo die* on a certain day *qui dies* which day *futurus esset* would be *ante diem sextum* the sixth day before *calendas Novembres* the calends of November? *Num me fefellit* did it escape my notice, *Catilina* Catiline, *non modo* not only *res* the fact itself *tanta* so

impo rtant, *tam atrox* so atrocious, *tam incredibile* so incredible, *verum* but, (*id quod* a thing which *est is multo magis admirandum* much more to be wondered at) *dies* the very day? *Ego idem* I also *dixi* said *in senatu* in the senate *te* that you *contulisse* fixed *cædem* the slaughter *optimatum* of the nobles *in ante-diem-sextum* for the sixth day before *calendas Novembres* the calends of November, *tum* at the time *quum* when *multi principes* many of our chief men *profugerunt* went away *Roma* from Rome *non tam* not so much *causa* for the sake *sui conservandi* of saving themselves *quam* as *tuorum consiliorum reprimendorum* of check-ing your designs. *Num potes* are you able *inficiari* to deny *te* that you, *illo ipso die* on that very day, *cir-cumclusum* hemmed in *meis præsidiis* by my guards, *mea diligentia* by my diligence, *non potuisse* were not able *commovere* to stir *te* yourself *contra rempublicam* against the republic, *quum* when *tu* you, *discessu* at the departure *cæterorum* of the rest, *dicebas* said *tamen* nevertheless *te* that you *esse contentum* were content *nostra cæde* with the slaughter of us *qui* who *remansis-semus* remained? 8. *Quid* what? *quum* when *tu* you *confideres* trusted *te* that you *occupaturum esse* would seize *Præneste* Præneste *calendis ipsis Novembribus* on the very calends of November *nocturno impetu* in an assault by night, *sensistine* did you [not] perceive *illam coloniam* that that colony *munitam esse* was fortified, *meo jussu* by my command, *præsidiis* with garrisons, *custodiis* with day watches, *vigiliis* and with night-watches? *Agis* you do *nihil* nothing, *moliris* you plan *nihil* nothing, *cogitas* you think of *nihil* nothing, *quod* which *ego* I *non modo* not only *non audiam* do not hear of, *sed etiam* but also *non videam* do not see *planeque sentiam* and know clearly.

IV. *Recognosce tandem* review now *mecum* with me *illam noctem superiorem* that night before ; *jam intelli-ges* you will at once see *me* that I *vigilare* am watching *multo acrius* much more actively *ad salutem* for the safety *quam* than *te* you *ad perniciem* for the destruc-

non reipublicæ of the reipublic. *Dico* I say *te* that you *venisse* came *priori nocte* the night before *inter falcarios* among the scythe-makers (*non agam* I will not deal with you *obscure* obscurely) *in domum* into the house *Marci Lææ* of Marcus Læca; *complures* that several persons *socios* your associates *ejusdem amentiæ* in the same folly *scelerisque* and wickedness *convenisse* came together *eodem* to the same place. *Num audes* do you dare *negare* deny it? *Quid* why *taces* are you silent? *Convincam* I will prove it *si* if *negas* you deny it? *Video enim* for I see *esse* that there are *hic* here *in senatu* in the senate *quosdam* some *qui* who *fuere* were *una* together *tecum* with you. 9. *O dii immortales* oh immortal gods! *ubinam gentium* where in the world *sumus* are we? *in qua urbe* in what city *vivimus* do we live? *quam rempublicam* what [kind of] republic *habemus* have we! *Hic* here, *sunt* there are *hic* here, *patres conscripti* conscript fathers, *in nostro numero* in our number, *in hoc* in this *sanctissimo* the most solemn *gravissimoque consilio* and grave assembly *orbis* of the globe *terræ* of the earth, *qui* [men] who *cogitent* are thinking *de meo interitu* about my death *nostrumque omnium* and [the death] of all of us, *qui* who are thinking *de exitio* about the destruction *hujus orbis* of this city *atque adeo* and moreover *orbis terrarum* of the whole earth. *Ego* I *consul* the consul *video* see *hosce* these men *et rogo* and ask them *sententiam* their opinion *de republica* about the republic; *et* and *nondum vulnero* do not yet wound *voce* with my words *eos* those *quos oportebat* who ought [long ago] *trucidari* to be slain *ferro* with the sword.

Fuisti igitur you were then, *Catilina* Catiline, *apud Læcam* at Læca's house *illa nocte* on that night: *distribuisti* you divided out *partes* the parts *Italiæ* of Italy: *statuisti* you fixed *quo* whither *placeret* it seemed good *quemque* that each *proficisci* should go: *delegisti* you chose *quos* whom *relinqueres* you should leave *Romæ* at Rome, *quos* whom *educeres* you should lead out *tecum* with you; *descripsisti* you marked out *artes* the parts *urbis* of the city *ad incendia* for setting on fire : *confirmasti* you assured them *te* that you *exiturum esse* would go forth *jam* at once : *dixisti* you said *esse* that it was *etiam nunc* even now, *paululum moræ* a little delay *tibi* to you *quod* that *ego* I *viverem* was alive. *Reperti sunt* there were found *duo equites Romani* two Roman knights, *qui* who *liberarent* freed *te* you *ista cura* from that care *et* and *pollicerentur* promised *sese* that they *interfecturos* would kill *me* me *paulo* a little *ante lucem* before dawn *illa ipsa nocte* that same night *in meo lectulo* in my bed. 10. *Ego* I *comperi* found out *hæc omnia* all these things *etiam* even *cœtu vestro* your assembly *vixdum dimisso* having scarcely yet been dismissed ; *munivi* I fortified *atque firmavi* and strengthened *domum meam* my house *majoribus præsidiis* with a greater guard : *exclusi* I shut out *eos* those *quos* whom *tu* you *miseras* had sent *ad me* to me *mane* in the morning *salutatum* to salute me, *quum* when *illi ipsi* those same men *venissent* had come *quos* whom *ego* I *jam prædixeram* had already foretold *multis* to many *ac summis viris* and most respectable men *esse* to be *venturos* about to come *ad me* to me *id temporis* at that time.

V. *Quæ* which things *quum ita essent* being so, *Catilina* Catiline, *perge* proceed *quo* whither *cœpisti* you have begun : *egredere* go out *aliquando* at last *ex urbe* from the city ; *portæ* the gates *patent* are open ; *proficiscere* set forth : *illa tua Manliana castra* that Manlian camp of yours *desiderant te* misses you *imperatorem* for its commander *nimium diu* too long ; *educ* lead out *tecum* with you *etiam omnes tuos* all your men also ; *si minus* if not [all], *quam plurimos* [yet] as many as possible ; *purga* purify *urbem* the city ; *liberabis me* you will free me *magno metu* from great fear *dummodo* provided that only *murus* the wall *intersit* intervene *inter me* between me *atque te* and you. *Non potes* you cannot *jam* now *versari* dwell *diutius* any longer *nobiscum* with us ; *non feram* I

8

will not bear it, *non patiar* I will not suffer it, *non sinam* I will not permit it. 11. *Magna gratia* great gratitude *habenda est* is to be felt *diis immortalibus* to the immortal gods *atque* and *huic Iovi Statori* to this Iupiter Stator, *antiquissimo custodi* the most ancient guard *hujus urbis* of this city, *quod* that *effugimus* we have escaped *jam* already *toties* so often *tam horribilem* so horrible *tamque infestam pestem* and so deadly a pest *reipublicæ* to the republic. *Summa salus* the general safety *reipublicæ* of the state *non est periclitanda* must not be endangered *sæpius* too often *in uno homine* on one man. *Quamdiu* as long as *insidiatus es* you plotted, *Catilina* Catiline, *mihi* against me *consuli designato* consul elect, *defendi* I defended *me* myself *non publico præsidio* not by a public guard, *sed* but *privata diligentia* by private diligence. *Quum* when *proximis comitiis consularibus* at the last consular comitia *voluisti* you wished *interficere* to slay *me* me *consulem* the consul *et* and *competitores tuos* your competitors *in Campo* in the campus [Martius], *compressi* I checked *tuos nefarios conatus* your wicked attempts *præsidio* with the protection *et copiis* and the resources *amicorum* of my friends *nullo tumultu* no tumult *concitato* having been stirred up *publice* publicly; *denique* lastly, *quotiescumque* as often as *petiisti me* you attacked me, *obstiti tibi* I resisted you *per me* by myself, *quamquam* although *videbam* I saw *perniciem meam* that my destruction *conjunctam esse* was joined *cum magna calamitate* with a great disaster *reipublicæ* of the republic. 12. *Nunc* now *jam petis* you are already attacking *universam rempublicam* the whole state *aperte* openly; *vocas* you are invoking *templa* the temples *deorum immortalium* of the immortal gods, *tecta* the houses *urbis* of the city, *vitam* the life *omnium civium* of all the citizens, *denique* and in short *totam Italiam* the whole of Italy *ad exitium* to destruction *et vastitatem* and waste.

Quare wherefore, *quoniam* since *nondum audeo* I do

not yet dare *facere* to do *id* that *quod* which *est* **k** *primum* the chief *atque* and *proprium* proper duty *hujus imperii* of this office *disciplinæque* and of the discipline *majorum* of our forefathers, *faciam* I will do *id* that *quod* which *est* is *lenius* more gentle *ad severitatem* in the way of severity *et* and *utilius* more useful *ad communem salutem* towards the common safety. *Nam* for *si* if *jussero* I shall have commanded *te* you *interfici* to be put to death, *reliqua manus* the rest of the band *conjuratorum* of conspirators *residebit* will settle down *in republica* in the state. *Sin* but if *tu* you *exieris* shall have gone forth (*quod* which *jamdudum* for some time *hortor te* I have been advising you to do) *sentina* the sink *tuorum comitum* of your companions *magna* great *et perniciosa* and destructive *reipublicæ* to the state *exhaurietur* will be drawn off *ex urbe* out of the city. 13. *Quid* what *est* is it, *Catilina* Catiline? *Num dubitas* do you hesitate *facere* to do, *me imperante* at my command, *id that quod* which *jam faciebas* you were already doing *tua sponte* of your own accord? *Consul* the consul *jubet* bids *hostem* an enemy *exire* to go forth *ex urbe* from the city. *Interrogas me* you ask me *num* is it *in exilium* to exile? *Non jubeo* I do not bid you, *sed* but, *si* ii *consulis me* you ask me, *suadeo* I advise you.

VI. Quid enim for what *est* is there, *Catilina* Catiline, *quod* which *possit* can *jam* now *delectare* delight *te* you *in hac urbe* to this city, *in qua* in which *est* there is *nemo* no one *extra istam conjurationem* besides that conspiracy *perditorum hominum* of abandoned men, *qui* who *non metuat te* does not fear you, *nemo* no one *qui* who *non oderit* does not hate you? *Qua nota* what mark *domesticæ turpitudinis* of domestic baseness *est* is there, *non inusta* that is not branded *vitæ tuæ* on your life? [*Quod dedecus* what disgrace *infamiæ* of the infamy *rerum privatarum* of your private affairs *non hæret* does not adhere to you?]

Quæ libid- what licentiousness *unquam abfuit* was ever absent *ab oculis* from your eyes, *quod facinus* what crime *unquam* ever *a manibus tuis* from your hands, *quod flagitium* what flagitiousness *a toto corpore* from your whole person? *Cui adolescentulo* to what young man *quem* whom *irretisses* you might have enticed *illecebris* by the allurements *corruptelarum* of corruptions, *non prætulisti* have you not proffered *aut* either *ferrum* a sword *ad audaciam* for audacity *aut facem* or a torch *ad libidinem* for lust? 14. *Quid vero* but what? *Nuper* lately, *quum* when *vacuefecisses* you had made vacant *domum* your house *novis nuptiis* for new nuptials *morte* by the death *superioris uxoris* of your former wife, *nonne cumulasti* did you not aggravate *hoc scelus* this crime *etiam* also *alio incredibili scelere* by another incredible crime? *Quod* which *ego* I *prætermitto* omit *et* and *facile* easily *patior* suffer *sileri* to be passed over in silence, *ne videatur* that there may not seem *aut* either *exstitisse* to have existed *aut* or *non vindicata esse* not to have been avenged *in hac urbe* in this city *immanitas* the atrocity *tanti facinoris* of so great a deed. *Prætermitto* I pass over *ruinas* the ruins *tuarum fortunarum* of your fortunes *quas omnes* all of which *senties* you will feel *impendere tibi* hang over you *proximis Idibus* on the next Ides; *venio* I come *ad illa* to those things *quæ* which *pertinent* relate *non* not *ad privatam ignominiam* to the private ignominy *tuorum vitiorum* of your vices, *non* not *ad domesticam tuam difficultatem* to your domestic difficulty *ac turpitudinem* and dishonour, *sed* but *ad summam vitam* to the general life *salutemque* and safety *reipublicæ* of the republic *atque* and *ad* to [the life and safety] *omnium nostrum* of all of us. 15. *Potestne* can *hæc lux* this light, *Catilina* Catiline, *aut* or *spiritus* the breath *hujus cæli* of this heaven *esse* be *jucundus* pleasant *tibi* to you, *quum scias* when you know *esse* that there is *nminem* no one *qui* who *nesciat* is ignorant *te* that you *pridie* on the day before *calendas Ianuarias* the calends of Ianuary, *Lepido et Tullo consulibus* in the consulship of Lepidus and Tullus, *stetisse* stood *in comitio* in the comitium *cum telo* with a weapon? *paravisse* that you got ready *manum* a band *causa* for the purpose *interficiendorum consulum* of slaying the consuls *et principum* and chief men *civitatis* of the state? *non mentem aliquam* that no wisdom *aut* or *timorem tuum* fear on your part *sed* but *fortunam* the fortune *reipublicæ* of the republic *obstitisse* was an obstacle *sceleri tuo* to your wickedness *ac furori* and madness? *Ac jam* and now *omitto* I pass over *illa* those matters, *neque enim* for neither *sunt* are [those aut obscura* either obscure *aut* or *non multa* not many *commissa* which were done *post* afterwards. *Quoties* how often *tu conatus es* have you attempted *interficere* to kill *me* me *designatum* when [consul] elect, *quoties* how often *consulem* when actual consul! *Quot tuas petitiones* how many of your attacks *ita conjectas* so aimed *ut* that *viderentur* they seemed *non posse* not to be able *vitari* to be avoided, *effugi* did I escape *parva quadam declinatione* by some slight movement *et* and, *ut* as *aiunt* they say, *corpore* with my body. *Agis* you do *nihil* nothing, *assequeris* you attain to *nihil* nothing, [*moliris* you design *nihil* nothing, *quod* which *valeat* is able *latere mihi* to escape me *in tempore* in due time]: *neque tamen* yet neither *desiistis* have you ceased *conari* to attempt *oc velle* and to hope. 16. *Quoties* how often *sica ista* has that dagger *jam* already *extorta est* been wrested *de manibus tibi* from your hands! *quoties vero* but how often *excidit* has it fallen from you *casu aliquo* by some chance *et elapsa est* and escaped! [*tamen* yet *non potes* you are not able *carere ea* be without it *diutius* any longer:] *quæ quidem wh*, [dagger] indeed, *quibus sacris* by what sacred *rites initiata sit* it has been initiated *ac devotata* and dedicated *nescio* I know not, *quod* because *putas* you think *it necesse* necessary *defigere* to fix it *in corpore* in the body *consulis* of the consul.

VII. *Nunc vero* but now, *quæ* what *est* is *ista tua vita* that life of yours! *Loquar enim* for I will speak *jam* now *tecum* with you *sic* so, *non* not *ut* that *videar* I may seem *esse permotus* to be influenced *odio* by hatred, *quo* by which *debeo* I ought [to be], *sed* but *ut* that [I may seem to be influenced] *misericordia* by pity *quæ nulla* which in no wise *debetur* is due *tibi* to you. *Venisti* you came *paulo ante* a little while ago *in senatum* into the senate; *quis* who *ex hac tanta frequentia* out of this great assembly, *ex tot tuis amicis* of so many friends of yours *ac necessariis* and connexions *salutavit te* saluted you? *Si* if *hoc* this *contigit* has happened *nemini* to no one *post memoriam* since the memory *hominum* of men, *expectas* do you await *contumeliam* the contempt *vocis* of their voice, *quum* when *sis oppressus* you are crushed *gravissimo judicio* by the weighty judgement *taciturnitatis* of their silence? *Quid* why [need I say], *quod* that *ista subsellia* those seats *vacuefacta sunt* were vacated *adventu tuo* at your approach? *quod* that *omnes* all *consulares* of consular rank *qui* who *persæpe* very often *constituti fuerunt* were marked out *tibi* by you *ad cædem* for slaughter, *reliqeurunt* left *istam partem* that part *subselliorum* of the benches *nudam* bare *atque inanem* and empty, *simul atque* as soon as *assedisti* you sat near them? *Quo animo* with what feeling *tandem* at length *putas* do you think *hoc* that this *ferendum* is to be borne *tibi* by you? 17. *Si* if *Hercle* by Hercules *servi mei* my slaves *metuerent* feared *me* me *isto pacto* in that manner, *ut* as *omnes cives tui* all your countrymen *metuunt* fear *te* you, *putarem* I should think *domum meam* that my house *relinquendam* ought to be abandoned: *tu non arbitraris* do you not think *urbem* that the city [ought to be left] *tibi* by you! *et* and, *si* if *viderem* I saw *me* myself *injuria* wrongfully *tam graviter suspectum s-*

grievously an object of suspicion *atque offensum* and offence *meis civibus* to my countrymen, *mallem* I would rather *me* that I *carere* should be without *aspectu* the sight *civium* of my countrymen *quam* than *conspici* be looked on *infestis oculis* by the hostile eyes *omnium* of all of them : *tu* you, *quum* although *conscientia* by the consciousness *tuorum scelerum* of your crimes *agnoscas* you recognize *odium* that the hatred *omnium* of all *justum* is just *et* and *jam* already *debitum* due *tibi* to you *diu* long ago, *dubitas* do you hesitate *vitare* to avoid *adspectum* the look *præsentiamque* and presence *eorum* of those men *quorum mentes* whose minds *sensusque* and feelings *vulneras* you are wounding? *Si* if *parentes tui* your parents *timerent* feared *atque odissent* and hated *te* you *neque posses* and you could not *placare* appease *eos* them *ulla ratione* in any manner, *ut* as *opinor* I think, *concederes* you would withdraw *aliquo* somewhither *ab eorum oculis* from their eyes : *nunc* now *patria* your country, *quæ* which *est* is *communis parens* the common parent *omnium uostrum* of all of us, *odit* hates *ac metuit* and fears *te* you, *et* and *jamdiu* already for a long time *nihil judicat* judges nothing *de te* about you *nisi* except *cogitare* that you are thinking *de parricidio suo* about murdering her. *Tu* will you *neque verebere* neither reverence *hujus auctoritatem* her authority, *neque sequere* nor abide by *judicium* her judgment, *neque pertimesces* nor fear *vim* her power? 18. *Quæ* [your country] which *agit* deals *sic* thus *tecum* with you, *Catilina* Catiline, *et* and *loquitur* speaks with you *quodammodo* after a manner *tacita* though silent: " *Nullum facinus* no crime *jam* now *aliquot annis* for several years *extitit* has shown itself *nisi* but *per te* by your agency : *nullum flagitium* no flagitiousness *sine te* without you : *tibi* to you *uni* alone *neces* the deaths *multorum civium* of many citizens, *tibi* to you *vexatio* the harassing *direptioque* and plundering *sociorum* of the allies *fuit* has been *impunita* with impunity *ac*

14

libera and free : *tu* you *valuisti* have prevailed *non so-lum* not only *ad negligendas leges* to neglect the laws, *ac quæstiones* and inquisitions *verum* but *etiam* also *ad evertendas* to overthrow *perfringendasque* and break through them. *Tuli tamen* I however put up with *superiora illa* those former doings, *ut potui* as I was able, *quamquam* although *fuerunt* they were *non fe-renda* such as ought not to have been borne : *nunc vero* but now *me* that I *esse* should be *totam* wholly *in metu* in fear *propter te unum* on account of you alone ; *quicquid* whatever *increpuerit* may have made a noise, *Catilinam* that Catiline *timeri* is the object feared ; *nullum consilium* that no counsel *videri* seems *posse* to be able *iniri* to be entered upon *contra me* against me *quod* which *abhorreat* is alien *a tuo scelere* from your wickedness—*non est* it is not *ferendum* to be borne. *Quamobrem* wherefore *discede* depart *atque* and *eripe* take away *hunc timorem* this fear *mihi* from me : *si* if *est* it is *verus* true, *ne opprimar* that I may not be crushed ; *sin* but if *falsus* false, *ut* that *tandem* at length *desinam* I may cease *aliquando* some time *timere* to fear."

VIII. 19. *Si* if, *ut* as *dixi* I said, *patria* your country *loquatur* speak *hæc* these words *tecum* with you, *nonne debeat* ought she not *impetrare* to obtain [her request] *etiam si* even if *non possit* she is not able *adhibere* to use *vim* force ? *Quid* why [need I say] *quod* that *tu* you *ipse* yourself *dedisti* have given *te* yourself *in custodiam* into custody ? *quid* why *quod* that *causa* for the sake *vitandæ suspicionis* of avoiding suspicion *dixisti* you said *te* that you *velle* wished *habitare* to dwell *apud Manium Lepidum* with Manius Lepidus ? *a quo* by whom *non receptus* not having been received *ausus es* you dared *venire* to come *etiam* also *ad me* to me, *atque* and *rogasti* you asked *ut* that *asservarem* I would keep *te* you *domi meæ* at my house. *Quum* when *tulisses* you had received *a me quoque* from me also *id responsum* this answer *me*

15

that I *posse* could *nullo modo* in no wise *esse* be *tuto* safely *iisdem paristibus* within the same house-walls, *qui essem* seeing that I was *in magno periculo* in great danger *quod* because *contineremur* we were contained *iisdem mœnibus* within the same city-walls, *venisti* you came *ad Quintum Metellum* to Quintus Metellus *prætorem* the prætor. *A quo* by whom *repudiatus* having been rejected *demigrasti* you went over *aa sodalem tuum* to your companion *virum optimum* that excellent man *Marcum Marcellum* Marcus Marcellus : *quem* whom *tu* you *videlicet* forsooth *putasti* thought *fore* to be about to be *et* both *diligentissimum* most diligent *ad custodiendum* to guard you *et* and *sagacissimum* most sagacious *ad suspicandum* to suspect *et* and *fortissimum* most brave *ad vindicandum* to avenge. *Sed* but *quam longe* how far *videtur* does it seem *debere* that [he] ought *abesse* to be absent *a carcere* from prison *atque* and *a vinculis* from chains *qui* who *jam* already *ipse* himself *judicarit se* has judged himself *dignum* worthy *custodia* of ward ? 20. *Quæ* which things *quum ita sint* being so, *Catilina* Catiline, *dubitas* do you hesitate, *si* if *non potes* you cannot *emori* die outright *hic* here *æquo animo* with equanimity, *abire* to depart *in aliquas terras* to some foreign lands or other, *et* and *mandare* to trust *fugæ* to flight *solitudinique* and to solitude *vitam istam* that life *ereptam* saved *multis suppliciis* from many punishments *justis* just *debitisque* and deserved ?

" *Refer* refer it," *inquis* you say, "*ad senatum* to the senate :" *postulas enim* for you demand *id* that *et* and *dicis* you say *si* [that] if *hic ordo* this order *decreverit* shall have decreed *placere* that it seems good *sibi* to them *te* that you *ire* should go *in exilium* into banishment, *te* you *esse obtemperaturum* will obey. *Non referam* I will not refer it to them, *et tamen* and yet *faciam* I will cause *ut* that *intelligas* you may perceive *quid* what *hi th***~~ ~~***tiant* think *de te* about you. *Egredere* go for~~ ~~ . *urbe* from the city. *Catilina*

16

Catiline, *libera* free *rempublicam* the republic *metu* from fear: *proficiscere* go *in exilium* into exile. *si* if *expectas* you are waiting for *hanc vocem* this word. *Quid est* what is it, *Catilina* Catiline? *Ecquid* what *attendis* are you waiting for? *Ecquid animadvertis* do you perceive *silentium horum* their silence? *Patiuntur* they allow you, *tacent* they are silent. *Quid* why *expectas* do you await *auctoritatem* the authority *loquentium* of [them] speaking, *voluntatem* the will *quorum* of whom *tacitorum* when silent *perspicis* you see clearly? 21. *At* but *si* if *dixissem* I had said *hoc idem* this same *huic optimo adolescentulo* to this excellent young man *Publio Sextio* Publius Sextius, *si* or if *fortissimo viro* to that brave man *Marco Marcello* Marcus Marcellus, *senatus* the senate *jam* already *jure optimo* with the greatest justice *intulisset* would have laid *vim* violence *et manus* and their hands *mihi* on me *consuli* the consul *in hoc ipso templo* in this very temple. *De te autem* but in your case, *Catilina* Catiline, *probant* they approve, *quum* when *quiescunt* they are silent; *quum* when *patiuntur* they are passive, *decernunt* they are giving a decision: *quum* when *tacent* they are silent, *clamant* they are clamorous: *neque hi* and not these *solum* only, *quorum auctoritas* whose authority *est* is *videlicet* it seems *cara* dear *tibi* to you, *vita* but whose life *vilissima* is of little value; *sed* but *etiam* also *illi equites Romani* those Roman knights *honestissimi* most honourable *atque optimi viri* and excellent men *ceterique fortissimi cives* and the other brave citizens, *qui* who *circumstant* are standing round *senatum* the senate, *quorum* of which *tu* you *potuisti* were able *et* both *videre* to behold *frequentiam* the number *et* and *perspicere* to see clearly *studia* the wishes *et* and *paulo ante* a little while ago *exaudire* to hear *voces* the voices, *quorum manus* whose hands *et tela* and weapons *ego* I *jamdiu* for some long time *vix* with difficulty *contineo* withheld *abs te* from you; *adducam* I will induce *eosdem* the same men *facile* without difficulty *ut prosequantur* to escort *te* you *usque* even *ad portas* to the gates *relinquentem* when you leave *hæc* these [places] *quæ* which *jampridem studes* you have long been desiring *vastare* to lay waste.

IX. 22. *Quanquam* and yet *quid* what *loquor* am I saying? *ut* [is it possible] that *ulla res* anything *frangat* can break *te* you? *ut* that *tu* you *unquam corrigas* should ever correct *te* yourself? *ut* that *tu* you *meditere* should meditate *ullam fugam* anything like flight? *ut* that *tu cogites* you should think of *ullum exilium* anything like exile? *Utinam* I wish *du immortales* that the immortal gods *duint tibi* may give you *istam mentem* such thoughts! *tametsi* although *video* I see, *si* if *perterritus* frightened *mea voce* by my voice *induxeris* you shall induce *animum* your mind *ire* to go *in exilium* into banishment, *quanta tempestas* what a storm *invidiæ* of odium *impendeat* hangs over *nobis* myself, *si minus* if not *in præsens tempus* for the present time, *memoria* the memory *scelerum tuorum* of your crimes *recenti* being fresh, *at* yet at all events *in posteritatem* among posterity. *Sed* but *est tanti* it is worth while *mihi* to me; *dummodo* if only *ista calamitas* that calamity *sit* be *privata* private *et* and *sejungatur* be separated *a periculis* from the dangers *reipublicæ* of the state. *Sed* but *ut* that *tu* you *commoveare* should be moved *tuis vitiis* by your own vices, *ut* that *pertimescas* you should fear *pænas* the punishments *legum* of the laws, *ut* that *cedas* you should yield *temporibus* to the occasions *reipublicæ* of the state, *non est postulandum* it is not to be demanded of you. *Neque enim* for neither *es* are you *is* such a man, *Catilina* Catiline, *ut* that *aut pudor* either shame *unquam revocarit* has ever recalled *te* you *a turpitudine* from baseness, *aut* or *metus* fear *a periculo* from danger *aut* or *ratio* reason *a furore* from madness. 28. *Quamobrem* wherefore, *ut* as *dixi* I have said *jam* already *sæpe* often *antea* before, *proficiscere* set forth ; *ac* and, *si* if *vis* you wish *con-flare* to kindle [as if with a pair of bellows] *invidiam* hatred *mihi* against me *inimico tuo* your enemy *ut* as *prædicas* you assert, *perge* go *recta* straightway *in exilium* into exile. *Vix feram* I shall scarcely endure *sermones* the talk *hominum* of men *si* if *feceris* you shall do *id* that : *vix sustinebo* I shall scarcely sustain *molem* the weight *istius invidiæ* of that odium *si* if *ieris* you shall go *in exilium* into exile *jussu* at the command *consulis* of the consul. *Sin autem* but if on the contrary *mavis* you would rather *servire* be of service *meæ laudi* to my praise *et gloriæ* and glory, *egredere* go forth *cum importuna manu* with that troublesome band *sceleratorum* of wicked men ; *confer te* betake yourself *ad Manlium* to Manlius ; *concita* stir up *perditos cives* those abandoned citizens ; *secerne* separate *te* yourself *a bonis* from the good ; *infer bellum* bring war upon *patriæ* your country; *exulta* triumph *impio latricinio* in your unholy brigand- age ; *ut* that *videaris* you may seem *isse* to have gone *non* not *ejectus* cast out *a me* by me *ad alienos* among strangers, *sed* but *invitatus* invited *ad tuos* to your own friends. 24. *Quanquam* although *quid* why *ego invitem* should I invite *te* you, *a quo* by whom *sciam* I know *jam* [that] already *esse præmissos* there have been sent forward *qui* [men] who *præstolarentur tibi* might wait for you *armati* armed *ad Forum Aurelium* at Forum Aurelium ? *cui* [you] for whom *sciam* I know *diem* that a day *pactam esse* has been bargained *et constitutam* and fixed on *cum Manlio* with Manlius ? *a quo* by whom *sciam* I know *etiam* also *argenteam illam aquilam* that that silver eagle, *quam* which *confido* I trust *futuram esse* will be *perniciosam* pernicious *et funestam* and fatal *tibi* to you *ac* and *omnibus tuis* to all your friends, *cui* for which *sacrarium* a shrine *scelerum tuorum* of your crimes *constitutum fuit* was established *domi tuæ* at your house ? *præmissam ess* has been sent in advance? *Ut* [is it likely] that *tu* you *possis* can *diutius* any longer *carere* be without *illa* that [eagle] *quam* which *solebas* you were accustomed *venerari* to worship, *proficiscens* when going out *ad cædem* to murder? *a cujus altaribus* from whose altars *sæpe transtulisti* you have often transferred *istam impiam dexteram* that impious right hand *ad necem* to the destruction *civium* of your countrymen?

X. 25. *Ibis* you will go *tandem* at length *aliquando* some time or other *quo* [to that place] whither *tua ista cupiditas* that covetousness of yours *effrenata* unrestrained *ac furiosa* and mad *jampridem te rapiebat* was long ago hurrying you. *Neque enim* for neither *hæc res* does this fact *affert* bring *dolorem* pain *tibi* to you, *sed* but *incredibilem quandam voluptatem* a certain incredible pleasure. *Natura* nature *peperit te* gave you birth *ad hanc amentiam* for this madness, *voluntas* [your own] choice *exercuit* has trained you, *fortuna* your fortune *servavit* has preserved you. *Tu* you *non modo* not only *nunquam concupisti* have never desired *otium* quiet, *sed* but *ne bellum quidem* not even war, *nisi* except *nefarium* a wicked one. *Nactus es* you have obtained *manum* a band *improborum* of wicked men *conflatam* formed *ex perditis* out of men ruined *atque derelictis* and abandoned *ab omni* by all *non modo* not only *fortuna* fortune, *verum* but *etiam spe* even hope. 26. *Qua lætitia* what pleasure *tu perfruere* will you enjoy *hic* here? *quibus gaudiis* in what delights *exsultabis* will you exult? *quanta in voluptate* in what great pleasure *bacchabere* will you revel, *quum* when *in tanto numero* in so great a number *tuorum* of your friends *neque audies* you will neither hear *neque videbis* nor see *quenquam bonum virum* any good man? *Illi labores tui* those labours of yours *qui* which *feruntur* are talked about, *meditati sunt* have been planned *ad studium* to the pursuit *hujus vitæ* of this life: *jacere* to lie *humi* on the ground *non modo* not only *ad ob-*

sidendum stuprum to effect a rape *verum* but *etiam*
also *ad facinus obeundum* to accomplish a crime ; *vigilare* to keep awake, *non solum* not only *insidiantem*
plotting *somno* against the sleep *maritorum* of hus-
bands, *verum* but *etiam* also *bonis* against the goods
occisorum of those you have slain. *Habes* you have
[an opportunity] *ubi* where *ostentes* you may show *illam præclaram tuam patientiam* that splendid en-
durance of yours *famis* of hunger, *frigoris* of cold,
inopiæ of the want *rerum omnium* of all things ; *quibus* by which *senties* you will feel *brevi tempore* in a
short time *te* that you *confectum esse* are done for.
27. *Profeci* I succeeded *tantum* so far *tum* at the time,
quum when *repuli* I rejected *te* you *a consulatu* from
the consulship, *ut* that *posses* you should be able *tentare* to make attempts on *rempublicam* the republic
exul as an exile *potius* rather *quam* than *vexare* to
harass it *consul* as consul ; *atque* and *ut* that *id quod*
that which *esset susceptum* had been undertaken *sce-
lerate* wickedly *a te* by you, *nominaretur* should be
named *latrocinium* brigandage *potius* rather *quam*
bellum than war.

XI. *Nunc* now, *patres conscripti* conscript fathers,
ut that *detester* I may denounce *ac deprecer* and de-
precate *a me* from myself *quandam querimoniam* a
kind of complaint *patriæ* of my country *prope justam*
which is almost well founded, *percipite* understand,
quæso I pray you, *diligenter* carefully *quæ* what
[words] *dicam* I say *et* and *mandate* commit *ea* them
penitus deeply *animis vestris* to your hearts *menti-
busque* and minds. *Etenim* for in truth, *si* if *patria*
my country *quæ* which *est* is *multo carior* much dearer
mihi to me *vita mea* than my life, *si* if *cuncta Italia*
all Italy, *si* if *omnis respublica* the whole republic
loquatur speak *sic* thus *mecum* with me, " *Marce
Tulli* Marcus Tullius, *quid* what *agis* are you doing ?
Tune patieris will you suffer *eum* that man *exire* to
go forth, *quem* whom *comperisti* you have discovered

21

esse to be *hostem* an enemy, *quem* whom *vides* you see *futurum* about to be *ducem* the leader *belli* of a war, *quem* whom *sentis* you perceive *expectari* to be expected *imperatorem* as commander in chief *in castris* in the camp *hostium* of the enemy, *auctorem* the author *sceleris* of the wicked deed, *principem* the chief *conjurationis* of the conspiracy, *evocatorem* the caller-out *servorum* of the slaves *et* and *civium perditorum* of abandoned citizens, *ut* so that *videatur* he may appear *non* not *emissus esse* to have been let out *ex urbe* from the city *abs te* by you, *sed* but *immissus* let in *in urbem* into the city? *Nonne imperabis* will you not order *hunc* him *duci* to be led *in vincula* to chains, *non* [will you] not *rapi* to be dragged *ad mortem* to death, *non* [will you] not *mactari* to be slain *summo supplicio* by the most severe punishment? 28. *Quid* what *tandem* at length *impedit te* hinders you? *Mosne* [is it] the custom *majorum* of our ancestors? *At* but *etiam privati* even private men *persæpe* very often *mulctarunt* have punished *morte* with death *perniciosos cives* mischievous citizens *in hac republica* in this commonwealth. *An leges* or is it the laws *quæ* which *rogatæ sunt* have been enacted *de supplicio* about the punishment *civium Romanorum* of Roman citizens? *At* but *ii* those *qui* who *defecerunt* have revolted *a republica* from the state *nunquam tenuerunt* have never held *jura* the rights *civium* of citizens *in hac urbe* in this city. *An times* do you fear *invidiam* the hatred *posteritatis* of posterity? *Refers vero* you repay truly *præclaram gratiam* noble gratitude *populo Romano* to the Roman people, *qui* who *extulit* raised *tam mature* at so early an age *ad summum imperium* to the highest command *per omnes gradus* through all the grades *honoris* of honour *te* you *hominem* a man *cognitum* known *per te* through yourself [alone] *nulla commendatione* by no recommendation *majorum* of ancestors, *si* if *propter invidiam* on account of odium *aut* or *motum* the fear *alicujus periculi* of any danger *negligis* you neglect *salutem* the safety *civium tuorum* of your countrymen. 29. *Sed* but *si* if *est* there is *quis metus* any fear *invidiæ* of odium, *num est* is *invidia* the odium *severitatis* of severity *ac fortitudinis* and of boldness *pertinescenda* to be feared *vehementius* more vehemently *quam* than *inertiæ* of inactivity *ac nequitiæ* and culpable remissness? *An existimas* do you think, *quum* when *Italia* Italy *vastabitur* shall be laid waste *bello* with war, *urbes* its cities *vexabuntur* shall be harassed, *tecta* its houses *ardebunt* shall be in flames, *te* that you *non tum conflagraturum* will not then burn *incendio* in a fire *invidiæ* of public odium?"

XII. *His sanctissimis vocibus* to these hallowed words *reipublicæ* of the commonwealth, *et mentibus* and to the reasonings *eorum hominum* of those men *qui* who *sentiunt* think *idem* the same, *ego* I *respondebo* will answer *pauca* a few words. *Si* if *ego judicarem* I judged *hoc* this, *patres conscripti* conscript fathers, *optimum* best *factu* to be done, *Catilinam* that Catiline *mulctari* should be punished *morte* with death, *non dedissem* I would not have given *usuram* the use *unius horæ* of one hour *gladiatori isti* to that gladiator *ad vivendum* to live. *Etenim* for also, *si* if *summi viri* those great men *et* and *clarissimi cives* illustrious citizens, *non modo* not only *non contaminarunt* did not pollute *se* themselves *sed* but *etiam* even *honestarunt* made themselves honourable *sanguine* by the blood *Saturnini* of Saturninus *et* and *Gracchorum* the Gracchi *et Flacchi* and Flaccus *et* and *superiorum complurium* many former men, *certe* surely *non erit* it will not be *verendum* an object of fear *mihi* to me, *ne quid invidiæ* lest any odium *redundaret* should redound *mihi* on me *in posteritatem* among posterity *hoc interfecto* from the slaying of this man *parricida* the murderer *civium* of his countrymen. *Quod si* but if *ea* that [odium] *impenderet mihi* were hanging over me *maxime* to the utmost, *tamen* yet *semper fui* I have always been *hoc animo* of this disposition *ut putarem*

23

as to think *invidiam* odium *partam* obtained *virtute*
by merit *gloriam* glory, *non invidiam* not odium.
30. *Quanquam* although *sunt* there are *in hoc ordine*
in this order *nonnulli* some *qui* who *aut* either *non*
videant do not see *ea* those things *quæ* which *immi-*
nent are impending *aut* or *dissimulent* dissemble *ea*
those *quæ* which *vident* they see : *qui* who *aluerunt*
have nourished *spem* the hope *Catilinæ* of Catiline
mollibus sententiis by mild sentiments, *corroborave-*
runtque and have strengthened *conjurationem nas-*
centem the growing conspiracy *non credendo* by not
believing it : *quorum auctoritatem* whose authority
sequuti following *multi* many *non solum improbi* not
only bad men, *verum* but *etiam* also *imperiti* ignorant
men *dicerent* would say *si* if *animadvertissem* I had
inflicted punishment *in hunc* on him, *factum esse* that
it was done *crudeliter* cruelly *et regie* and tyranni-
cally. *Nunc* now *intelligo* I see *si* [that] if *iste* he
pervenerit shall arrive *in castra Manliana* at the camp
of Manlius, *quo* whither *intendit* he is setting out,
fore there will be *neminem* no one *tam stultum* so
foolish, *qui non videat* as not to see *conjurationem* that
a conspiracy *factam esse* has been made, *neminem* no
one *tam improbum* so wicked *qui non fateatur* as not
to acknowledge it. *Hoc autem uno* but he alone *in-*
terfecto having been put to death, *intelligo* I see *hanc*
pestem that this bane *reipublicæ* of the commonwealth
posse may *reprimi* be checked *paulisper* for a while,
non not *comprimi* be crushed *in perpetuum* for ever.
Quod si but if *ejecerit* he shall have cast out *se* himself *eduxeritque* and led out *secum* with him *suos* his
companions *et* and *aggregaverit* assembled together
eodem to the same place *cæteros naufragos* the other
shipwrecked fellows collected *undique* from all sides.
non modo not only *hæc pestis* this pest *reipublicæ* of
the republic *tam adulta* so full-grown *extinguetur* will
be extinguished *atque* and *delebitur* be destroyed.

24

verum but *etiam* also *stirps* the stem *ac semen* and seed *malorum omnium* of all these evils.

XIII. 31. *Etenim* for also, *patres conscripti* conscript fathers, *jamdiu versamur* we have now been long *in his periculis* amid these perils *conjurationis* of conspiracy *insidiisque* and plots ; *sed* but *nescio* I know not *quo pacto* in what manner, *maturitas* the fulness *omnium scelerum* of all crimes *ac* and *veteris fuoris* of ancient madness *et audaciæ* and audacity *erupit* has burst forth *in tempus* upon the time *nostri consulatus* of our consulship. *Quod si* but if *iste* he *unus* alone *tolletur* shall be taken away *ex tanto latrocinio* from this great set of brigands *videbimur* we shall seem *fortasse* perhaps *relevati esse* to have been freed *cura* from care *et metu* and fear *ad breve quoddam tempus* for a certain short time, *periculum autem* but danger *residebit* will settle down *et* and *erit inclusum* be included *penitus* deeply *in venis* in the veins *atque* and *in visceribus* in the bowels *reipublicæ* of the republic. *Ut* as *homines* men *ægri* sick *morbo gravi* of a severe disease *sæpe* often, *quum* when *jactantur* they are tossed about *æstu* by heat *febrique* and fever, *si* if *biberint* they have drunk *aquam gelidam* cold water, *videntur* seem *primo* at first *relevari* to be relieved, *deinde* and then *afflictantur* are afflicted *multo gravius* much more seriously *vehementiusque* and vehemently, *sic* so *hic morbus* this disease *qui* which *est* is *in republica* in the state, *relevatus* lightened *pœna* by the punishment *istius* of that man *ingravescet* will press down *vehementius* more weightily, *vivis reliquis* if the others are alive. 32. *Quare* wherefore, *patres conscripti* conscript fathers, *improbi* let the bad men *secedant* withdraw ; *secernant* let them separate *se* themselves *a bonis* from the good ; *congregentur* let them be congregated *in unum locum* into one place ; *denique* in short, *id quod* a thing which *sæpe dixi* I have often said *jam* already, *secernantur* let them be separated *a nobis* from us *muro* by the city-wall , *desinant* let them cease *insidiari* to plot *consuli* against the consul *domi suæ* at his own house, *circumstare* to stand round *tribunal* the tribunal *prætoris urbani* of the city prætor, *obsidere* to besiege *curiam* the senate-house *cum gladiis* with swords, *comparare* to prepare *malleolos* brushwood *et faces* and torches *ad inflammandam urbem* to fire the city ; *denique* lastly *sit inscriptum* let it be inscribed *in fronte* on the forehead *uniuscujusque* of each one *quid* what *sentiat* he thinks *de republica* about the state. *Polliceor* I promise *hoc* this *vobis* to you, *patres conscripti* conscript fathers, *fore* that there shall be *tantam diligentiam* such great diligence *in nobis* in us *consulibus* the consuls, *tantam auctoritatem* such great authority *in vobis* in you, *tantam virtutem* such great virtue *in equitibus Romanis* in the Roman knights, *tantam consensionem* such great consent *in omnibus bonis* in all good men, *ut videatis* that you will see *omnia* that all things *patefacta esse* have been laid open, *illustrata* brought to light, *oppressa* crushed, *vindicata* and punished *profectione* by the departure *Catilinæ* of Catiline.

33. *Hisce ominibus* with these omens, *Catilina* Catiline, *cum summa salute* with the general safety *reipublicæ* of the state *et* and *cum peste* with plague *ac pernicie tua* and destruction to yourself, *cumque exitio* and with the destruction *eorum* of those *qui* who *junxerunt* have joined *se* themselves *tecum* with you, *omni scelere* in every kind of wickedness *parricidisque* and felony, *proficiscere* set forth *ad impium* to your impious *ac nefarium bellum* and wicked war. *Tum* then *tu* thou, *Jupiter* Jupiter, *qui* who *constitutus es* wast established *a Romulo* by Romulus *iisdem auspiciis* by the same auspices *quibus hæc urbs* as this city, *quem* whom *vere nominamus* we truly name *Statorem* the Stator [Steadier] *hujus urbis* of this city *atque imperii* and empire, *arcebis* shalt forbid *hunc* him *et hujus socios* and his allies *a tuis aris* from thy altars *cæterisque templis* and the other temples, *a tectis* from

the houses *ac mœnibus* and walls *urbis* of the city, *a vita* from the life *fortunisque* and fortunes *civium omnium* of all the citizens, *et* and *mactabis* pursue *æternis suppliciis* with everlasting punishments *vivos* alive *mortuosque* and dead *omnes inimicos* all the enemies *bonorum* of good men *hostes* enemies *patriæ* of their country *latrones* robbers *Italiæ* of Italy, *conjunctos* leagued *inter se* among themselves *fœdere* in a confederacy *scelerum* of crimes *ac* and *nefaria societate* in an infamous alliance.

CATILINE II.

I. *Tandem aliquando* by this time at length, **Quirites** Romans, *vel ejecimus* we have either cast out *ex urbe* from the city *Lucium Catilinam* Lucius Catiline *furentem* raging *audacia* with audacity, *anhelantem* breathing *scelus* crime, *nefarie* wickedly *molientem* planning *pestem* the destruction *patriæ* of his country, *vinitantem* threatening *ferrum* sword *flammamque* and flames *vobis* against you *atque huic urbi* and this city, *vel* or *emisimus* we have sent him away, *vel* or *prosequuti sumus* we have pursued *verbis* with words *ipsum* himself *egredientem* departing. *Abiit* he is gone, *excessit* he has left us, *evasit* he has escaped, *erupit* he has burst forth ; *nulla pernicies* no destruction *a monstro illo* from that monster *atque prodigio* and prodigy *jam comparabitur* will now be prepared *intra mœnia* within the walls *mœnibus ipsis* for the walls themselves. *Atque* and *vicimus* we have defeated *sine controversia* without doubt *hunc quidem* him indeed *unum ducem* the single leader *hujus belli domestici* of this domestic war. *Sica enim illa* for that dagger *non jam versabitur* will not now have place *intra latera nostra* within our sides ; *non pertimescemus* we shall not fear *in Campo* in the Campus [Martius], *non in foro* nor in the forum, *non in cu-*

27

ria nor in the senate-house, *non denique* nor lastly, *intra domesticos parietes* within the walls of our houses. *Ille* he *motus est* was removed *loco* from his place, *quum* when *depulsus est* he was driven forth *ex urbe* from the city. *Jam geremus* we shall now carry on *justum bellum* a just war *cum hoste* with an enemy, *nullo impediente* no one preventing us. *Sine dubio* without doubt *perdidimus* we ruined *hominem* the man, *vicimusque* and defeated him *magnifice* magnificently, *quum* when *conjecimus* we cast *illum* him *ex occultis insidiis* from his secret plottings *in apertum latrocinium* into open brigandage. 2. *Quod vero* but that *non extulit* he did not bear forth *mucronem* his blade *cruentum* bloody *ut* as *voluit* he wished, *quod* that *egressus est* he went out *vivis nobis* leaving us alive, *quod* that *extorsimus* we wrested *ferrum* the sword *de manibus ei* out of his hands, *quod* that *reliquit* he left *cives* the citizens *incolumes* safe, *quod* that [he left] *urbem* the city *stantem* standing, *quanto mærore* with what great sorrow *putatis* do you think *illum* that he *esse* is *afflictum* afflicted *et profligatum* and discomfited? *Ille* he *nunc* now *jacet* lies *prostratus* prostrate, *Quirites* Romans, *et* and *sentit* feels *se* that he *esse perculsum* is struck down *atque abjectum* and cast out, *et* and *sæpe* often *retorquet* turns back *oculos* his eyes *profecto* in truth *ad hanc urbem* to this city, *quam* which *luget* he mourns *ereptam esse* to have been snatched *ex faucibus suis* out of his jaws; *quæ quidem* which indeed *videtur* seems *mihi* to me *lætari* to rejoice, *quod* that *evomuerit* it has vomited forth *projeceritque* and cast *foras* out of its doors *tantam pestem* such a great pest.

II. 3. *At* but *si* if *est* there is *quis* any one *talis* such a man *quales* such as *omnes oportebat* all ought *esse* to be, *qui* who *vehementer accuset* vehemently accuses *me* me *in hoc ipso* in this very matter *in quo* in which *mea oratio* my speech *exultat* exults *et triumphat* and triumphs, *quod* that *non comprehenderim*

I have not seized *tam capitalem hostem* so capital an enemy *potius* rather *quam emiserim* than let him go; *ista* that, *Quirites* Romans, *non est* is not *mea culpa* my fault, *sed* but *temporum* [the fault] of the times. *Oportebat Lucium Catilinam* Lucius Catiline ought *jampridem* long ago *interremptum esse* to have been slain *et affectum* and treated *gravissimo supplicio* with the severest punishment, *idque* and that *et* both *mos* the custom *majorum* of our forefathers *et severitas* and the strictness *hujus imperii* of this my office *et respublica* and the republic *postulabat* demanded *o me* of me. *Sed* but *quam multos* how many *putatis de* you think *fuisse* there were *qui* who *non crederent* did not believe *quæ* what *ego deferrem* I reported? *quam multos* how many *qui* who *propter stultitiam* from folly *non putarent* did not think so? *quam multos* how many *qui* who *etiam* even *defenderent* defended him? *quam multos* how many *qui* who *propter improbitatem* from depravity *faverent* favoured him? *Ac si* and if, *illo sublato* when he was removed, *judicarem* I judged ← *omne periculum* that all danger *depelli* would be warded off *a vobis* from you, *ego* I *jampridem* long ago *sustulissem* would have cut off *Lucium Catilinam* Lucius Catiline *periculo* at the risk *non modo* not only *invidiæ meæ* of my being hated *verum* but *etiam* also *vitæ meæ* of my life. 4. *Sed* but *quum viderem* when I saw, *re* the truth *etiam tum* even then *probata* having been proved *ne vobis quidem* not even to all of you, *si* that if *mulctassem* I had punished *illum* him *morte* with death *ut* as *meritus erat* he had deserved, *fore* it would result *ut* that *oppressus* weighed down *invidia* by odium *non possem* I should not be able *persequi* to follow up *socios ejus* his confederates, *deduxi* I brought *rem* the matter *huc* to this point *ut* that *possetis* you might be able *tum* then *palam* openly *pugnare* to fight, *quum* when *videretis* you saw *hostem* the enemy *aperte* openly: *quem hostem* which enemy *uidem* indeed, *Quirites* Romans, *quam vehementer* how very much *ego putem* I think *esse* to be *veren-dum* an object of dread *foris* abroad, *licet intelligatis* it is allowed you to see *hinc* from this fact, *quod* that *etiam fero* I even bear *moleste* with displeasure *illud* this, *quod* that *exierit* he has gone out *parum comitatus* thinly attended *ex urbe* from the city. *Utinam* I wish *ille* he *eduxisset* had led out *secum* with him *omnes suas copias* all his forces. *Eduxit* he led out *mihi* [as must be granted] me *Tongilium* Tongilius, *quem* whom *cœperat* he had begun *amare* to love *in prætexta* whilst still wearing the prætextate robe, *Publicium* Publicius *et Munatium* and Munatius, *quorum æs alienum* whose debt, *contractum* contracted *in popina* in the cookshop *poterat* was able *afferre* to bring about *nullum motum* no disturbance *reipublicæ* of the commonwealth : *reliquit* he left behind—*quos viros* what men ! *quanto ære alieno* in what great debt [sunk] ! *quam valentes* how strong ! *quam nobiles* how noble !

III. 5. *Itaque* therefore *ego* I *et* both *Gallicanis legionibus* with our Gallic legions *et* and *hoc delectu* with this levy *quem* which *Quintus Metellus* Quintus Metellus *habuit* had *in Piceno* in the Picenian *et Gallico agro* and Gallic territory, *et* and *his copiis* with these forces *quæ* which *quotidie* daily *comparantur* are brought together *a nobis* by us, *magnopere contemno* greatly despise *illum exercitum* that army *collectum* gathered *ex senibus desperatis* out of desperate old men, *ex agresti luxuria* of rural debauchery, *ex rusticis decoctoribus* of rustic melters down of their property, *ex iis* of those *qui* who *maluerunt* would rather *deserere* desert *vadimonia* their bail *quam* than *illum exercitum* that army ; *quibus* to whom *non modo* not only *si* if *ego* I *ostendero* shall show *aciem* the line *nostri exercitus* of our army, *verum etiam* but even if [I shall show] *edictum* the edict *prætoris* of the prætor, *concident* they will collapse. *Hos* these men *quos* whom *video* I see *v̇⸲⸲⸲e* flitting about *in foro* in the forum, *quos* whom *stare* standing *ad curiam* about the senate-house, *quos* whom *etiam venire* even coming *in senatum* into the senate, *qui* who *nitent* are sleek *unguentis* with perfumes, *qui* who *fulgent* shine *purpura* in purple, *mallem* I would rather *eduxisset* he had led out *suos milites* these his soldiers *secum* with him: *qui* who *si* if *permanent* [they] continue to remain *hic* here *mementote* remember *esse* that it is *non tam* not so much *illum exercitum* that army *quam* as *hos* these men *qui* who *deseruerunt* have deserted *exercitum* the army, *pertimescendos* who are to be feared *nobis* by us. *Atque* and *etiam* also *sunt* they are *magis* more *timendi* to be feared *hoc* on this account, *quod* that *sentiunt* they feel *me* that I *scire* know *quid* what *cogitent* they are devising *neque tamen permoventur* and yet are not moved. 6. *Video* I see *cui* to whom *Apulia* Apulia *sit attributa* has been assigned, *qui* who *habeat* has *Etruriam* Etruria, *qui* who *agrum Picenum* the Picenian territory *qui* who *Gallicum* the Gallic, *qui* who *depoposcerit* has claimed *sibi* for himself *has urbanas insidias* these city plots *cædis* of murder *atque incendiorum* and conflagration. *Sentiunt* they perceive *omnia consilia* that all the plans *superioris noctis* of the former night *delata esse* have been reported *ad me* to me: *patefeci* I made them known *hesterno die* yesterday *in senatu* in the senate: *Catilina* Catiline *ipse* himself *pertimuit* trembled, *profugit* fled: *quid* what *hi* do these *expectant* wait for? *Næ* in truth *illi* they *vehementer errant* greatly err, *si* if *sperant* they hope *meam pristinam lenitatem* that my former lenity *futuram* will be *perpetuam* everlasting.

IV. *Jam sum assequutus* I have now obtained *quod* what *expectavi* I have waited for, *ut* that *vos* you *videretis* might see *conjurationem* that a conspiracy *factam esse* was made *aperte* openly *contra rempublica* against the state. *nisi vero* unless indeed, *si* if *est* there is *quis* any one *qui* who *non putat* does not think *similes* that those who are like *Catilinæ* to Catiline *sentire* think *cum Catilina* with Catiline. *Non est* there is not *jam* now *locus* room *lenitati* for lenity, *res ipsa* the thing itself *flagitat* demands *severitatem* severity. *Etiam nunc* even now *concedam* I will grant *unum* one thing : *exeant* let them depart, *proficiscantur* let them set forth, *ne patiantur* that they may not suffer *Catilinam miserum* the wretched Catiline *tabescere* to pine *desiderio* at the want *sui* of them. *Demonstrabo* I will point out *iter* the road : *profectus est* he set out *via Aurelia* on the Aurelian road : *si* if *volent* they shall be willing, *consequentur* they will reach him *ante vesperam* before evening. 7. *O fortunatam rempublicam* oh fortunate republic, *si quidem* if indeed *ejecerit* it shall have cast out *hanc sentinam* this sink *hujus urbis* of this city ! *Uno Catilina* Catiline alone, *mehercule* so may Hercules protect me ! *exhausto* being drained off, *respublica* the state *videtur* seems *mihi* to me *relevata* relieved *et recreata* and restored. *Quid enim mali* for what evil *aut sceleris* or wickedness *potest* can *fingi* be imagined *aut* or *excogitari* be devised *quod* which *ille* he *non conceperit* has not conceived ? *Quis veneficus* what poisoner *tota Italia* in the whole of Italy, *quis gladiator* what gladiator, *quis latro* what robber, *quis sicarius* what assassin, *quis parricida* what murderer, *quis subjector* what substituter *testamentorum* of wills, *quis circumscriptor* what swindler, *quis ganeo* what debauchee, *quis nepos* what prodigal, *quis adulter* what adulterer, *quæ mulier infamis* what infamous woman, *quis corruptor* what corrupter *juventutis* of youth, *quis corruptus* what corrupted man, *quis perditus* what desperado *potest* can *inveniri* be found, *qui* who *non fateatur* does not confess *se* that he *vixisse* has lived *familiarissime* most familiarly *cum Catilina* with Catiline ? *Quæ cædes* what murder *facta est* has taken place *per hosce annos* during these [late] years *sine illo* without him? *quod nefarium stuprum* what wicked rape *non* not [committed] *per illum* through him?   8. *Jam vero* but now *quæ illecebra* what temptation *juventutis* of youth *fuit* was there *unquam* ever *tanta* so great *in ullo homine* in any man *quanta* as *in illo* in him? *qui* who *ipse* himself *amabat* loved *alios* others *turpissime* most disgracefully *serviebat* and was subservient *flagitiosissime* most flagitiously *amori* to the love *aliorum* of others : *aliis* to some *pollicebatur* he used to promise *fructum* the enjoyment *libidinum* of their lusts, *aliis* to others *mortem* the death *parentum* of their parents, *non modo* not only *impellendo* by instigating *verum* but *etiam* also *adjuvando* by helping them.   *Nunc vero* but now *quam subito* how suddenly *collegerat* had he collected *ingentem numerum* a great number *perditorum hominum* of desperate men *non solum* not only *ex urbe* out of the city, *verum etiam* but also *ex agris* out of the fields! *Fuit* there was *nemo* no one, *non modo* not only *Romæ* at Rome, *sed* but *nec* neither *in ullo angulo* in any corner *totius Italiæ* of the whole of Italy, *oppressus* overwhelmed *ære alieno* by debt, *quem* whom *non adsciverit* he did not enlist *ad hoc incredibile fœdus* in this incredible league *sceleris* of crime.

V.   9. *Atque* and *ut* that *possitis* you may be able *perspicere* to see through *ejus diversa studia* his different exertions *in dissimili ratione* in different occupations, *est* there is *nemo* no one *in ludo gladiatorio* in the school of gladiators *paulo audacior* at all more audacious [than usual] *ad facinus* to commit crime *qui* who *non fateatur* does not confess *se* that he *est* is *intimum* the intimate friend *Catilinæ* of Catiline; *nemo* no one *in scena* on the stage *levior* more fickle *et nequior* and more wicked [than usual] *qui* who *non commemoret* does not boast *se* that he *fuisse* has been *prope* almost *sodalem* the companion *ejusdem* of the same [Catiline].   *Atque tamen* and yet *idem* the same man *assuefactus* practised *exercitatione* in the exercise *stuprorum* of rapes *et scelerum* and crimes, *prædicabatur* was proclaimed *ab istis* by those men *fortis* as brave *perferendis frigore* in bearing cold *et siti* and thirst *ac vigiliis* and night-watches, *quum* whilst *consumeret* he was wasting *subsidia* the aids *industriæ* of industry *atque instrumenta* and instruments *virtutis* of virtue *in libidine* on lust *audaciaque* and audacity. 10. *Si vero* but if *sui comites* his companions *sequuti fuerint* shall have followed *hunc* him, *si* if *flagitiosi greges* those disgraceful bands *desperatorum hominum* of desperate men *exierint* shall have gone forth *ex urbe* from the city, *O beatos nos* oh happy we, *O fortunatam rempublicam* O fortunate republic, *O præclaram laudem* O splendid praise *mei consulatus* of my consulship! *Libidines enim* for the lusts *hominum* of men *jam* now *non sunt* are not *mediocres* moderate, *non* not *audaciæ* [savouring] of audacity *humanæ* common to human nature *ac tolerandæ* and to be tolerated: *cogitant* they devise *nihil* nothing *nisi cædes* but murder, *nisi incendia* but conflagration, *nisi rapinas* but plunder: *profuderunt* they have squandered *patrimonia sua* their patrimonies, *abligurierunt* they have licked up *fortunas suas* their fortunes: *res* property *jampridem* long ago *cœpit* has begun *deficere eos* to fail them, *nuper* and lately *fides* credit: *tamen* yet *illa eadem libido* that same licentiousness, *quæ* which *erat* was [theirs] *in abundantia* in [the time of their] abundance, *permanet* remains. *Quod si* but if *quærerent* they sought after *comessationes* feastings *solum* only *et scorta* and harlots *in vino* amidst their drinking *et alea* and diceing, *illi quidem* they indeed *essent* would be *desperandi* men lost to hope, *sed tamen* but yet *essent* they would be *ferendi* such as we might put up with. *Quis vero* but who *possit* could *ferre* put up with *hoc* this, *inertes homines* that such idle fellows *insidiari* should plot *fortissimis viris* against the bravest

34

men, *stultissimos* the most foolish *prudentissimis* against the wisest, *ebriosos* drunkards *sobriis* against the sober, *dormientes* sluggards *vigilantibus* against the watchful? *qui* who, *mihi* grant me! *accubantes* reclining *in conviviis* at banquets, *complexi* embracing *mulieres impudicas* immodest women, *languidi* languid *vino* with wine, *confecti* knocked up *cibo* with eating, *redimiti* crowned *sertis* with garlands, *obliti* smeared *unguentis* with ointments, *debilitati* enfeebled *stupris* with rapes, *eructant* belch forth *sermonibus suis* in their talk *cædem* the slaughter *bonorum* of good men *atque* and *incendia* the firing *urbis* of the city. 11. *Quibus* over whom *ego confido* I trust *fatum aliquod* that some fate *impendere* is impending *et pœnas* and penalties *jamdiu* already for a long time *debitas* due *improbitati* to their knavery, *nequitiæ* worthlessness, *sceleri* wickedness, *libidini* and licentiousness, *aut* or *jam* already *instare* is threatening them *plane* plainly *aut* or *certe* at all events *appropinquare* is approaching. *Quos* whom *si* if *meus consulatus* my consulship *sustulerit* shall have got rid of, *quoniam* since *non potest* it cannot *sanare* cure them, *propagarit* it will have lengthened out *non* not *breve tempus* a short space *nescio quod* I know not what, *sed* but *multa secula* many ages *reipublicæ* to the republic. *Est enim* for there is *nulla natio* no nation *quam pertimescamus* for us to fear; *nullus rex* no king, *qui* who *possit* is able *facere bellum* to make war *populo Romano* on the Roman people. *Omnia externa* all foreign affairs *pacata sunt* have been quieted *terra* by land *marique* and by sea *virtute* by the valour *unius* of one man. *Domesticum bellum* a domestic war *manet* remains: *intus* within *sunt* are *insidiæ* plots; *periculum* the danger *inclusum est* is enclosed *intus* within: *hostis* the enemy *est* is *intus* within; *certandum est nobis* we have to contend *cum luxuria* with luxury, *cum amentia* with madness, *cum scelere* with wickedness.

35

Ego profiteor I profess *me* myself, *Quirites* Romans, *ducem* leader *huic bello* for this war : *suscipio* I undertake *inimicitias* the enmities *hominum perditorum* of these abandoned men. *Quæ* whatever things *poterunt* will be possible *sanari* to be healed, *sanabo* I will heal *quacunque ratione* in whatever manner I can ; *quæ* whatever things *erunt* shall be *resecanda* to be cut away, *non patiar* I will not suffer *manere* to remain *ad perniciem* to the destruction *civitatis* of the state. *Proinde* therefore *aut exeant* either let them go out *aut* or *quiescant* be quiet : *aut* or *si* if *permanent* they remain *et* both *in urbe* in the city *et* and *in eadem mente* in the same temper, *expectent* let 'nem expect *ea* those things *quæ* which *merentur* they deserve.

VI. 12. *At* but, *Quirites* Romans, *etiam sunt* there also are *qui* some who *dicant* say *Catilinam* that Catiline *ejectum esse* has been cast out *a me* by me *in exilium* into exile. *Quod* which *si* if *ego* I *possem* could *assequi* obtain *verbo* by a word, *ejicerem* I would cast out *istos ipsos* those same men *qui* who *loquuntur* speak *hæc* these things. *Homo* the man *videlicet* forsooth *timidus* timid *et permodestus* and over modest *non potuit* could not *ferre* bear *vocem* the voice *consulis* of the consul ; *simul atque* as soon as *iussus est* he was bidden *ire* to go forth *in exilium* into exile, *ivit* he went forth. *Quum* when *pæne interfectus essem* I had been almost slain *domi meæ* at my house *hesterno die* in the course of yesterday, *vocavi* I called *senatum* the senate *in ædem* into the temple *Jovis Statoris* of Jupiter Stator : *detuli* I reported *rem omnem* the whole matter *ad patres conscriptos* to the conscript fathers. *Quo* whither *quum* when *Catilina* Catiline *venisset* had come *quis senator* what senator *appellavit eum* addressed him ? *quis* who *salutavit* saluted him ? *quis* who *denique* in short *adspexit* looked on him *ita* in the same way *ut* as *perditum civem* a lost citizen *ac* and *non potius* not rather *ut* as *importunissimum hostem* a most malignant enemy? *Quin etiam* but moreover *principes* the chiefs *ejus ordinis* of that order *reliquerunt* left *nudum* bare *atque inanem* and empty *illam partem* that part *subselliorum* of the benches *ad quam* to which *ille* he *accesserat* had approached. 13. *Hic* upon this *ego* I, *vehemens ille consul* that vehement consul, *qui* who *ejicio* cast out *cives* citizens *in exilium* into exile *verbo* by a word, *quæsivi* asked *a Catilina* of Catiline, *an* whether *fuisset* he had been *apud Marcum Læcam* at the house of Marcus Læca *nocturno conventu* at the night-meeting *necne* or not. *Quum* when *ille* he, *homo audacissimus* a most impudent fellow, *convictus* convicted *conscientia* by conscience, *primo* at first *reticuisset* had kept silence, *patefeci* I unfolded *cætera* the rest; *edocui* I explained fully *quid* what *egisset* he had done *ea nocte* that night, *ubi* where *fuisset* he had been, *quid* what *constituisset* he had arranged *in proximam* for the next [night], *quemadmodum* how *ratio* the scheme *totius belli* of the whole war *descripta esset* had been marked out *ei* for him. *Quum* when *hesitaret* he hesitated, *quum* when *teneretur* he was caught, *quæsivi* I asked *quid* why *dubitaret* he hesitated *proficisci* to set out *eo* thither *quo* whither *jampridem pararat* he had long prepared [to go]; *quum* since *scirem* I knew *arma* that arms, *quum* since *secures* that axes, *quum* since *tubas* that trumpets, *quum* since *signa militaria* that military ensigns, *quum* since *aquilam illam argenteam* that the silver eagle, *cui* for which *ille* he *etiam* also *fecerat* had made *sacrarium* a sanctuary *scelerum* of crimes *domi suæ* at his own house, *præmissam esse* had been sent on beforehand. 14. *Ejiciebam* was I casting out *in exilium* into exile, *quem* him whom *videbam* I saw *jam* already *ingressum esse* to have entered *in bellum* on war? *Et enim* for moreover *credo* I believe, *Manlius iste* that Manlius *centurio* the centurion, *qui* who *posuit* placed *castra* his camp *in agro Fæsulano* in the Fæsulan territory, *indixit*

37

declared *bellum* war *suo nomine* in his own name *po-pulo Romano* against the Roman people : *et* and *illa castra* that camp *nunc* now *non expectant* is not waiting for *Catilinam* Catiline *ducem* as its general : *et ille* and he, *ejectus* cast out *in exilium* into exile, *conferet se* will betake himself, *ut* as *aiunt* they say, *Massiliam* to Marseilles, *non* not *in hæc castra* to this camp.

VII. *O conditionem miseram* oh for the wretched lot *non modo* not only *administrandæ* of administering, *verum* but *etiam* even *conservandæ reipublicæ* of saving a state! *Nunc* now, *si* if *Lucius Catilina* Lucius Catiline *circumclusus* hemmed in *ac debilitatus* and weakened *meis consiliis* by my counsels, *laboribus* labours, *periculis* and dangers, *subito* suddenly *pertimuerit* shall have become alarmed, *mutaverit* and changed *sententiam* his opinion, *deseruerit* deserted *suos* his friends, *abjecerit* and cast aside *consilium* his design *belli faciundi* of making war, *converterit* and shall have changed *iter* his path *ex hoc cursu* from this course *sceleris* of crime *et belli* and war *ad fugam* to flight *atque* and *in exilium* into exile, *ille* he *dicetur* will be said *non* not *spoliatus esse* to have been stripped *a me* by me *armis* of the weapons *audaciæ* of his audacity, *non* not *obstupefactus* astounded *ac perterritus* and thoroughly frightened *mea diligentia* by my diligence, *non* not *depulsus* driven *de spe* from his hope *conatuque* and enterprise, *sed* but *indemnatus* uncondemned, *innocens* innocent, *ejectus esse* to have been cast out *in exilium* into exile *a consule* by the consul *vi* by violence *et minis* and threats ; *et* and *erunt* there will be *qui* [men] who *velint* wish *illum* him, *si* if *fecerit* he shall do *hoc* this, *existimari* to be thought *non* not *improbrum* criminal *at miserum* but unfortunate ; *me* [and] me *non* not *diligentissimum consulem* a most active consul, *sed* but *crudelissimum tyrannum* a most cruel tyrant. 15. *Est* it is *tanti* worth while *mihi* for me, *Quirites* Romans, *subire* to encounter *tempestatem* the storm *hujus falsæ* of this false *atque* and *iniquæ invidiæ* unjust odium, *dummodo* provided that *periculum* the peril *hujus horribilis* of this horrible *ac nefarii belli* and wicked war *depellatur* be warded off *a vobis* from you. *Dicatur* let him be said *sane* in truth *ejectus esse* to have been cast out *a me* by me, *dummodo* provided that *eat* he goes *in exilium* into exile. *Sed* but *credite* believe me, *non est iturus* he does not intend to go. *Ego* I, *Quirites* Romans, *nunquam optabo* shall never wish *a diis immortalibus* of the immortal gods, *causa* for the sake *levandæ meæ invidiæ* of lightening my own odium, *ut* that *audiatis* you may hear *Lucium Catilinam* that Lucius Catiline *ducere* is leading *exercitum* an army *hostium* of enemies *atque volitare* and hovering about us *in armis* in arms : *sed tamen* but yet *audietis* you will hear it *triduo* in three days, *timeoque* and I fear *illud* this *multo magis* much more *ne* lest *sit* it be *aliquando* at some time or other *invidiosum* a cause of odium *mihi* against me, *quod* that *emiserim illum* I have let him go *potius* rather *quam* than *quod* that *ejecerim* I have expelled him. *Sed* but *quum* since *sint* there are *homines* men *qui* who *dicant* say *illum* that he *ejectum esse* was cast out, *quum* inasmuch as *profectus sit* he has gone, *quid* what *iidem dicerent* would the same men say, *si* if *interfectus esset* he had been put to death? 16. *Quanquam* although *isti* those, *qui* who *dictitant* keep saying *Catilinam* that Catiline *ire* is going *Massiliam* to Marseilles *non tam* do not so much *queruntur* complain of *quam* as *verentur* fear *hoc* this. *Est* there is *nemo* no one *istorum* of them *tam misericors* so merciful, *qui* who *non malit* would not rather *illum* that he *ire* should go *ad Manlium* to Manlius *quam* than *ad Massilienses* to the people of Marseilles : *ille autem* but he, *si* if *Mehercule* by Hercules, *nunquam cogitasset* he had never thought of *hoc* this *quod* which *agit* he is doing *ante* before, *tamen* yet *mallet* would rather *se* that himself *inter-fici* should be killed *latrocinantem* whilst practising his favourite career of brigandage *quam* than *vivere* live *exulem* as an exile. *Nunc vero* but now, *quum* when *nihil* nothing *adhuc* as yet *acciderit* has happened *ei* to him *præter ipsius volentatem* contrary to his own wish *cogitationemque* and intention, *nisi* except *quod* that *profectus est* he has set out *Roma* from Rome *vivis nobis* whilst we are alive, *optemus* let us wish *potius* rather *quam* than *queramur* complain, *ut eat* that he may go *in exilium* into exile.

VIII. 17. *Sed* but *cur* why *loquimur* do we speak *tamdiu* so long *de uno hoste* about one enemy ? *et* and *de eo hoste* about that enemy, *qui* who *jam* already *fatetur* confesses *se* that he *esse* is *hostem* an enemy *et* and *quem* whom *non timeo* I do not fear *quia* because, *quod* what *semper volui* I have always wished, *murus* the city wall *interest* lies between us ; *dicimus* [but] say *nihil* nothing *de his* about those *qui* who *dissimulant* dissemble, *qui* who *remanent* remain *Romæ* at Rome, *qui* who *sunt* are *nobiscum* with us ? *Quos* whom *quidem* indeed *ego I studeo* desire, *si* if *possit* it can *fieri* be done *ullo modo* in any manner, *non* not *tam* so much *ulcisci* to punish *quam* as *sanare* to cure *et* and *placare* to reconcile *ipsos* them *reipublicæ* to the state ; *neque* nor *intelligo* do I understand *quare* why *id* that *non possit* cannot *fieri* be done *si* if *volent* they will be willing *audire me* to hear me. *Exponam enim* for I will explain *vobis* to you, *Quirites* Romans, *ex quibus generibus* of what classes *hominum* of men *istæ copiæ* those forces *comparentur* are procured ; *deinde* then *afferam* I will bring *singulis* to each *medicinam* the medicine *consilii* of my counsel *atque* and *orationis meæ* of my oratory, *si* if *potero* I shall be able [to bring] *quam* any.

18. *Est* there is *unum genus* one class *eorum* of those *qui* who *in magno ære alieno* in great debt, *habent* have *etiam* also *majores possessiones* greater

possessions, *quorum amore* by the love of which *ad-ducti* influenced *possunt* they can *nullo modo* by no means *dissolvi* be dissolved. *Species* the appearance *horum hominum* of these men *est* is *honestissima* most respectable; *sunt enim* for they are *locupletes* wealthy: *voluntas vero* but their intention *et causa* and their cause *impudentissima* is most impudent. *Tu sis* can you be *ornatus* furnished *et copiosus* and abounding *agris* in land, *tu ædificiis* in buildings, *tu argento* in silver, *tu familia* in family, *tu omnibus rebus* in all things, *et dubites* and can you hesitate *detrahere* to detract *de possessione* from your property, *acquirere* and to gain *ad fidem* in your credit? *Quid enim* for what *expectas* do you expect? *Bellum* war? *Quid ergo* what then? *Putas* do you think *tuas possessiones* that your possessions *futuras* will be *sacrosanctus* sacred *in vastatione* amid the devastation *omnium* of all things? *An* or do [you expect] *tabulas novas* new tables [cancelling of debts]? *Errant* they err *qui* who *expectant* expect *istas* them *a Catilina* from Catiline? *Tabulæ novæ* new tables *proferentur* will be put forth *meo beneficio* by my good service *verum* but *auctionariæ* referring to an auction. *Neque enim* for neither *possunt* can *isti* those *qui* who *habent* have *possessiones* possessions, *esse* be *salvi* safe *alia ratione* in any other manner. *Quod* which *si* if *voluissent* they had been willing *facere* to do *maturius* sooner, *neque* and not (*id quod* a thing which *est* is *stultissimum* most foolish) *certare* to struggle *cum usuris* against usury *fructibus* by the produce *prædiorum* of their farms, *uteremur* we should use *his* these men *et* both *locupletioribus* richer *et* and *melioribus civibus* better citizens. *Sed* but *puto* I think *hosce homines* these men *minime* very little *pertimescendos* to be feared, *quod* because *aut* either *possunt* they may *deduci* be turned *de sententia* from their opinion, *aut* or *si* if *permanebunt* they shall abide in it, *videntur* they seem *mihi* to me *facturi* likely to make *vota* vows *magis* more *quam* than *arma laturi* to bear arms *contra rempublicam* against the republic.

IX. *Alterum genus* a second class *est* consists *eorum* of those *qui* who *quanquam* although *premuntur* they are oppressed *ære alieno* with debt, *tamen* yet *expectant* are waiting for *dominationem* power, *volunt* [who] wish *potiri* to obtain possession *rerum* of power; *arbitrantur* and think *se* that they *posse* can *consequi* obtain *perturbata republica* when the state is disturbed *honores* the honours *quos* which *desperant* they despair [of obtaining] *quieta* when it is quiet. *Quibus* to whom *hoc* this *videtur* seems *præcipiendum* needful to be told, *scilicet* indeed *unum* the one *et idem* and the same thing *quod* which [should be told] *cæteris omnibus* to all the others, *ut* in order that *desperent* they may cease to hope *se* that they *posse* can *consequi* obtain *id* that *quod* which *conantur* they are attempting; *primum* first *omnium* of all *me ipsum* that I myself *vigilare* am watchful, *adesse* am at hand, *providere* and am providing *reipublicæ* for the republic: *deinde* in the next place *esse* that there is *magnos animos* great courage *in bonis viris* in good men, *magnam concordiam* great concord, *maximam multitudinem* a very great multitude *præterea* and moreover *magnas copias* a great force *militum* of soldiers; *denique* lastly *deos immortales* that the immortal gods *præsentes* present with us *laturos esse* will bring *auxilium* aid *huic invicto populo* to this unconquered people, *clarissimo imperio* illustrious empire *pulcherrimæ urbi* and beautiful city, *contra tantam vim* against so great a power *sceleris* of wickedness. *Quod si* but supposing that *jam adepti sint* they have already obtained *id* that *quod* which *cupiunt* they desire *cum summo furore* with the greatest fury: *num illi sperant* do they hope, *in cinere* amidst the ashes *urbis* of the city *et sanguine* and the blood *civium* of the citizens, *quæ* which *concupierunt* they have desired *vor:-scelerata* with wicked *ac* and *nefaria mente* nefarious mind, *se* that they *futuros* will become *consules* consuls *ac dictatores* and dictators *aut* or *etiam reges* even notables? *Non vident* do they not see *se* that they *cupere* desire *id* that *quod* which *si* if *adepti fuerint* they shall obtain, *sit necesse* it will be necessary *concedi* that it be granted *fugitivo alicui* to some fugitive *aut gladiatori* or gladiator? 20. *Tertium genus* the third class *est* is *jam* already *affectum* touched *ætate* with age, *sed tamen* but yet *robustum* strong *exercitatione* by exercise : *quo ex genere* of which class *est* is *ipse Manlius* Manlius himself, *cui* to whom *Catilina* Catiline *nunc* now *succedit* succeeds. *Hi* these *sunt* are *homines* men *ex iis coloniis* out of those colonies, *quas* which *Sulla* Sulla *constituit* established *Fæsulis* at Fæsulæ ; *quas universas* all of which *ego sentio* I know *esse* to consist *civium optimorum* of the best citizens *et* and *fortissimorum virorum* of the bravest men. *Sed tamen* but yet *hi* these *sunt* are *coloni* colonists *qui* who *jactarunt* have boasted *se* themselves *sumptuosius* sumptuously *insolentiusque* and insolently *in insperatis* in unexpected *repentinisque pecuniis* and sudden money. *Dum* whilst *hi* these *ædificant* build houses *ut beati* like rich men, *dum* whilst *delectantur* they delight in *prædiis* farms, *lecticis* sedan-chairs, *familiis magnis* large families of slaves, *conviviis* and banquets *apparatis* laid out. *inciderunt* they have fallen *in tantum æs alienum* into such great debt *ut* that, *si* if *velint* they wish *esse* to be *salvi* safe, *Sulla* Sulla *sit excitandus* must be raised up by them *ab inferis* from the dead ; *qui* who *etiam* also *impulerunt* have driven *nonnullos agrestes* some rustics *tenues* small *atque* and *egentes homines* needy men *in eandem illam spem* to [have] that same hope *veterum rapinarum* of former plunder. *Quos utrosque* both of whom, *Quirites* Romans, *ego pono* I place *in eodem genere* in the same class *pro:-*

aatorum of robbers *direptorumque* and plunderers. *Sed* but *moneo hos* I warn these of *hoc* this : *desinant* let them desist *furere* to rage *ac cogitare* and to think about *proscriptiones* proscriptions *et dictaturas* and dictatorships. *Tantus enim dolor* for such great grief *illorum temporum* of those times *inustus est* is branded *civitati* into the city, *ut* that *non modo* not only *homines* men *sed* but *ne pecudes quidem* not even cattle *videantur* seem *mihi* to me *jam* now *esse* to be *passuræ* likely to suffer *ista* them.

X. 21. *Quartum genus* the fourth class *sane* in truth *est* is *varium* varied *et mixtum* and mixed *et turbulentum* and turbulent, *qui* who *jam* already *pridem premuntur* have long been overwhelmed ; *qui* who *nunquam emergent* will never rise again ; *qui* who *partim* partly *inertia* from sloth, *partim* partly *gerendo negotio* by managing their business *male* ill, *partim* partly *etiam* also *sumptibus* by expenses, *vacillant* are fluctuating *in vetere ære alieno* in old debt, *qui* who *defatigati* worn out *vadimoniis* y bails, *judiciis* trials, *proscriptionibus* and by proscriptions *bonorum* of goods, *dicuntur* are said *permulti* in great numbers *conferre se* to be taking themselves *in illa castra* into that camp *et* both *ex urbe* out of the city *et* and *ex agris* out of the fields. *Ego* I *arbitror* think *hosce* them *esse* to be *non tam* not so much *acres milites* bold soldiers *quam* as *inficiatores lentos* lazy repudiators [of debts]. *Qui homines* which men *primum* first *si* if *non possunt* they are not able *stare* to stand, *corruant* may fall, *sed* but *ita* in such a manner *ut* that *non modo* not only *civitas* the city *sed* but *ne vicini quidem proximi* not even their next neighbours *sentiant* may know it. *Nam* for *non intelligo* I do not understand *illud* this, *quamobrem* for what reason, *si* if *non possunt* they cannot *vivere* live *honeste* honestly, *velint* they wish *perire* to perish *turpiter* basely ; *aut* or *cur* why *arbitrentur* they think *se* that they *perituros* will perish *cum multis* in company with many

44

minore dolore with less pain *quam* than *si* if *pereant* they perish *soli* alone. 22. *Quintum genus* the fifth class *est* consists *parricidarum* of parricides, *sicario- rum* of cut-throats, *denique* in short *omnium facino- rosorum* of all [kinds of] evil-doers ; *quos* whom *ego* I *non revoco* do not recall *a Catilina* from Catiline *Nam* for *neque* neither *possunt* can they *divelli* be separated *ab eo* from him ; *et* and *pereant* let them perish *sane* forsooth *in latrocinio* in their brigandage, *quoniam* since *sunt* they are *ita multi* so many, *ut* that *carcer* a prison *non possit* cannot *capere eos* contain them. *Postremum autem genus* but the last class *est* is, *non solum* not only [last] *numero* in number, *ve- rum etiam* but also *genere ipso* in their kind *atque vita* and life ; *quod* which *proprium est* is the peculiar [class] *Catilinæ* of Catiline ; *de ejus delectu* of his own choice ; *immo vero* nay indeed *de complexu ejus* of his embrace *ac sinu* and bosom ; *quos* whom *vide- tis* you see *pexo capillo* with combed hair, *nitidos* sleek, *aut* either *imberbes* beardless *aut* or *bene barba- tos* thickly bearded, *tunicis* in vests *manicatis* having sleeves *et talaribus* and reaching to the ancles, *amic- tos* clothed *velis* with veils *non togis* not with togas, *quorum vitæ* of whose life *omnis industria* all the in- dustry *et labor* and toil *vigilandi* of watching *expro- mitur* is spent *in cœnis antelucanis* on suppers until just before daylight. 23. *In his gregibus* in these companies *versantur* abide *omnes aleatores* all gam- blers, *omnes adulteri* all adulterers, *omnes impuri* all the impure *impudicique* and immodest. *Hi pueri* these boys *tam lepidi* so witty *ac delicati* and deli- cate *didicerunt* have learnt *non solum* not only *amare* to love *et* and *amari* to be loved *neque* nor *cantare* to sing *et saltare* and to dance, *sed* but *etiam* also *vibrare* to brandish *sicas* knives *et* and *spargere* to dissemi- nate *venena* poisons : *qui* who *nisi* unless *exeunt* they go away, *nisi* unless *pereunt* they perish, *etiam si* even if *Catilina* Catiline *perierit* shall perish, *scitote* know *hoc* that this *futurum* will be *seminarium Catilinarium* a school for Catilines *in republica* in the republic. *Verum tamen* but however *quid* what *isti miseri* do those miserable men *volunt* wish *sibi* for themselves? *Num sunt ducturi* are they about to lead *secum* with them *suas mulierculas* their women *in castra* to their camp? *Quemadmodum autem* yet how *poterunt* will they be able *carere illis* to do without them, *praesertim* especially *jam* now *his noctibus* in such nights as these? *Quo autem pacto* but in what manner *illi perferent* will they endure *Apenninum* the Appennine *atque* and *illas pruinas* those frosts *ac nives* and snows? *Nisi* unless *putant* they think *se* that they *toleraturos* will endure *hiemem* the winter *facilius* the more easily *idcirco* for this reason *quod* because *didicerunt* they have learnt *saltare* to dance *nudi* naked *in conviviis* at their banquets?

XI. 24. *O bellum* oh war *magnopere* greatly *pertimescendum* to be feared, *quum* seeing that *Catilina* Catiline *habiturus sit* will have *hanc cohortem praetoriam* this praetorian cohort *scortorum* of strumpets! *Instruite nunc* draw up now, *Quirites* Romans, *vestra praesidia* your garrisons *vestrosque exercitus* and your armies *contra* against *has praeclaras copias* these illustrious troops *Catilinae* of Catiline; *et primum* and first *opponite* oppose *vestros consules* your consuls *imperatoresque* and commanders-in-chief *gladiatori illi* to that gladiator *confecto* worn out *et saucio* and wounded: *deinde* then *educite* lead forth *florem* the flower *ac robur* and strength *totius Italiae* of the whole of Italy *contra* against *ejectam illam* that outcast *ac debilitatam manum* and enfeebled band *naufragorum* of shipwrecked men; *urbes vero* but the cities *coloniarum* of the colonies *ac* and *municipiorum* of the municipal towns *jam respondebunt* will at once answer *tumulis silvestribus* to the wooded mounds *Catilinae* of Catiline. *Neque vero* but neither *debeo* ought I *conferre* to compare *caeteras copias* the other troops, *ornamenta* equipments, *præsidia vestra* and garrisons of yours *cum inopia* with the want *atque egestate* and poverty *illius latronis* of that robber. 25. *Sed* but, *si* if *omissis his rebus omnibus* omitting all these things, *quibus* in which *nos* we *suppeditamus* are sufficient, *ille* [but which] he *eget* is in need of, *senatu* senate, *equitibus Romanis* Roman knights, *populo* people, *urbe* city, *ærario* treasury, *vectigalibus* revenues, *cuncta Italia* all Italy, *provinciis omnibus* all the provinces, *exteris nationibus* and foreign nations; *si* if, *omissis his rebus* omitting these things, *velimus* we wish *contendere* to contrast *ipsas causas* the causes themselves, *quæ* which *confligunt* are conflicting *inter se* with one another, *possumus* we are able *intelligere* to understand *ex eo ipso* from that very thing *quam valde* how thoroughly *illi* they *jaceant* are lying on the ground. *Ex hac enim parte* for on one side *pudor* shame *pugnat* fights, *illinc* on the other side *petulantia* petulance; *hinc* on this side *pudicitia* chastity, *illinc* on that side *stuprum* fornication; *hinc* on this side *fides* honour, *illinc* on the other side *fraudatio* fraud; *hinc* on this side *pietas* piety, *illinc* on the other side *scelus* crime; *hinc* on this side *constantia* firmness, *illinc* on the other side *furor* madness; *hinc* on this side *honestas* honour, *illinc* on that *turpitudo* disgrace; *hinc* on this side *continentia* continence, *illinc* on that *libido* lust, *denique* lastly *æquitas* equity, *temperantia* temperance, *fortitudo* fortitude, *prudentia* prudence, *virtutes omnes* and all virtues, *certant* contend *cum iniquitate* with iniquity, *cum luxuria* with luxury, *cum ignavia* with sloth, *cum temeritate* with rashness, *cum vitiis omnibus* an with all the vices; *postremo* lastly *copia* plenty *cu egestate* with want, *bona ratio* a good system c *perdita* with a ruined one, *mens sana* a sound m *cum amentia* with madness, *denique* lastly *bona* good hope *confligit* conflicts *cum desperatione* despair *omnium rerum* of every thing. *In certa*

in a contest *ac prœlio* and battle *hujusmodi* of this
sort, *etiam si* even if *studia* the zeal *hominum* of men
deficiant fail us, *nonne* [will] not *dii immortales* the
immortal gods *ipsi* themselves *cogent* compel it, *tot*
that so many *et tanta vitia* and such great vices *su-
perari* should be overcome *ab his prœclarissimis vir-
tutibus* by these brilliant virtues?

XII. 26. *Quœ* which things *quum ita sint* being so,
Quirites Romans, *vos* you *defendite* defend *vestra
tecta* your homes *custodiis* with guards *vigiliisque* and
watches *quemadmodum* as *jam* [you have] already
antea before: *mihi* for me *consultum est* care has been
taken *ac provisum* and provision made *ut* that *esset*
there should be *satis prœsidii* enough protection *urbi*
for the city *sine vestro motu* without your being disturbed *ac* and *sine ullo tumultu* without any tumult.
Coloni omnes vestri all your colonists *municipesque*
and municipal townsmen *facti certiores* having been
informed *a me* by me *de hac nocturna excursione* of
this nocturnal sally *Catilinœ* of Catiline *facile de-
fendent* will easily defend *urbes suas* their cities
finesque and territories; *gladiatores* the gladiators,
quam which *ille* he *putavit* thought *fore* would be
maximam the greatest *et* and *certissimam manum* most
certain band *sibi* for him, *quanquam* although *sunt*
they are *meliore animo* of a better frame of mind
quam than *pars* part *patriciorum* of the patricians,
tamen yet *continebuntur* will be restrained *nostra potestate* by our power. *Quintus Metellus* Quintus Metellus, *quem* whom *ego* I *prospiciens* foreseeing *hoc*
this *prœmisi* sent forward *in Gallicanum* into the
Gallic *Picenumque agrum* and Picenian territory,
aut either *opprimet* will crush *hominem* the man, *aut*
or *prohibebit* will prevent *omnes ejus motus* all his
movements *conatusque* and attempts. *Reliquis autem
de rebus* but concerning the other matters *constitu-
endis* to be appointed, *maturandis* to be matured,
agendis and to be done, *jam referemus* we will at once

refer it *ad senatum* to the senate *quem* which *videtis* you see *vocari* to be called together.

27. *Nunc* now *illos* those, *qui* who *remanserunt* have remained *in urbe* in the city, *atque* and *adeo* moreover *qui* who *relicti sunt* have been left *in urbe* in the city *a Catilina* by Catiline *contra salutem* contrary to the safety *urbis* of the city *omniumque vestrum* and all of you, *quanquam* although *sunt* they are *hostes* enemies, *tamen* yet *quia* because *nati sunt* they were born *cives* citizens, *volo* I wish *eos* them *monitos* warned *etiam atque etiam* again and again. *Si* if *mea lenitas* my clemency *visa est* has seemed *cui* to any one *adhuc* still *solutior* too lax, *expectavit* it waited for *hoc* this, *ut* that *id* the thing, *quod* which *latebat* was lying hid, *erumperet* should break forth. *Quod* what *reliquum est* is remaining, *non possum* I cannot *jam* now *oblivisci* forget, *hanc* that this *esse* is *meam patriam* my country, *me* that I *esse* am *consulem* the consul *horum* of these, *mihi aut vivendum esse* that I either must live *cum his* with them *aut* or *moriendum* must die *pro his* for them. *Nullus est custos* there is no guard *portæ* of the gate, *nullus insidiator* no plotter *viæ* of their road; *si qui* if any of them *volunt* wish *exire* to go out, *possunt* they are able *consulere* to provide *sibi* for themselves; *qui vero* but whoever *commoverit* shall stir *se* himself *in urbe* in the city, *cujus* of whom *ego* I *deprehendero* shall detect *non modo* not only *factum ullum* any deed *sed* but *inceptum* any beginning *conatumve* or attempt *contra patriam* against our country, *sentiet* he shall feel *esse* that there are *consules* consuls *vigilantes* watching *in hac urbe* in this city, *esse* that there are *egregios magistratus* illustrious magistrates, *esse* that there is *fortem senatum* a brave senate, *esse* that there are *arma* arms, *esse* that there is *carcerem* a prison, *quem* which *majores nostri* our forefathers *voluerunt* intended *esse* to be *vindicem* the punisher *nefariorum*

of nefarious *ac manifestorum scelerum* and detect,*d* crimes.

XIII. 28. *Atque* and *hæc omnia* all these things *sic agentur* shall so be done, *Quirites* Romans, *ut* that *res maximæ* the most important matters *minimo motu* with the least commotion. *pericula summa* the greatest dangers *nullo tumultu* with no tumult, *intestinum* an intestine *ac* and *domesticum bellum* a domestic war *crudelissimum* the most cruel *ac maximum* and the greatest *post memoriam* since the memory *hominum* of men *sedetur* shall be put an end to, *me uno* I alone *togato* a civilian *duce* being the leader *et imperatore* and commander-in-chief: *quod* which [war] *ego* I, *Quirites* Romans, *sic administrabo* will so administer *ut* that, *si* if *poterit* it shall be possible *fieri* for it to be done *ullo modo* in any manner, *ne improbus quidem quisquam* not even any wicked man *sufferat* may suffer *pœnam* the punishment *sui sceleris* of his crime *in hac urbe* in this city. *Sed* but *si* if *vis* the force *manifestæ audaciæ* of manifest audacity, *si* if *periculum* the danger *impendens* impending *patriæ* over our country *deduxerit me* shall lead me away *necessario* of a necessity *de hac lenitate* from this lenity *animi* of disposition, *profecto* certainly *perficiam* I shall effect *illud* this, *quod* which *in tanto* in so great *et* and *tam insidioso bello* so insidious a war *videtur* seems *vix* scarcely *optandum* to be hoped, *ut* that *neque* neither *bonus quisquam* any good man *intereat* shall perish, *vosque* and you *omnes* all *jam* now *possitis* can *esse* be *salvi* safe *pœna* with the punishment *paucorum* of a few. **29.** *Quæ quidem* which things indeed *ego* I *polliceor vobis* promise you, *Quirites* Romans, *fretus* relying *neque* neither *mea prudentia* on my prudence *neque* nor *humanis consiliis* on human counsels, *sed* but *multis* on many *et* and *non dubiis significationibus* not doubtful intimations *deorum immortalium* of the immortal gods, *quibus ducibus* which being my guides *ingressus sum* I have

50

entered *in hanc spem* upon this hope *sententiamque* and opinion, *qui* [the gods] who *defendunt* are defending *sua templa* their temples *atque* and *tecta* the houses *urbis* of the city *non jam* not now *procul* from a distance *ab externo* from a foreign *atque* and *longinquo hoste* a distant enemy, *sed* but *hic* here *præsentes* being present, *suo numine* with their auspices *atque auxilio* and help : *quos* whom *vos* you, *Quirites* Romans, *debetis* are bound *precari* to pray to, *venerari* to worship *atque implorare* and to implore, *ut* that, *omnibus copiis superatis* having overcome all the forces *hostium* of enemies *terra* by land *marique* and by sea, *defendunt* they will defend *a nefario scelere* from the abominable wickedness *perditissimorum civium* of the most abandoned citizens, *hanc urbem* this city, *quam* which *voluerunt* they have chosen *esse* to be *pulcherrimam* the most beautiful, *florentissimam* the most flourishing *potentissimamque* and the most powerful.

CATILINE III.

I. 1. *Videtis* you see *hodierno die* this day, *Quirites* Romans, *rempublicam* the republic *vitamque* and the life *omnium vestrum* of you all, *bona* your goods, *fortunas* fortunes, *conjuges* wives, *liberosque vestros* and your children, *atque* and *hoc domicilium* this home *clarissimi imperii* of a most illustrious empire, *fortunatissimam* a most fortunate *pulcherrimamque urbem* and most beautiful city, *summo amore* by the great love *deorum immortalium* of the immortal gods *erga vos* towards you, *meis laboribus* by my labours, *consiliis* plans *periculisque* and dangers *ereptam* snatched *ex flamma* from flame *atque ferro* and sword *ac* and *pæne* almost *ex faucibus* from the jaws *fati* of fate *et conservatam* and preserved *ac restitutam* and restored *vobis* to you. 2. *Et* and, *si*

51

if *ii dies* those days *quibus* on which *conservamur* we
are saved *sunt* are *non minus jucundi* no less pleasant
nobis to us *atque illustres* and illustrious *quam* than
illi those *quibus* on which *nascimur* we are born,
quod because *est* there is *lætitia certa* a certain joy
salutis at one's safety, *conditio* [whereas] the lot
nascendi of being born *incerta* is uncertain, *et* and
quod because *nascimur* we are born *sine sensu* without feeling. *servamur* [but] are preserved *cum voluptate* with pleasure : *profecto* without a doubt,
quoniam since *sustulimus* we have raised *benevolentia*
by our good will *famaque* and by fame *ad deos immortales* to the immortal gods *illum* him *qui* who
condidit built *hanc urbem* this city, *is* that man *qui*
who *servavit* has saved *eandem hanc urbem* this same
city *conditam* built *amplificatamque* and amplified
debebit will be bound *esse* to be [held] *in honore* in
honour *apud vos* among you *posterosque vestros* and
your descendants. *Nam* for *restinximus* we have put
out *ignes* the fires *prope jam subjectos* that were almost already laid under *circumdatosque* and placed
round *toti urbi* the whole city, *templis* the temples,
delubris shrines, *tectis* houses *mœnibusque* and walls,
iidemque and we also *retudimus* have beaten back
gladios the swords *districtos* that had been drawn
in rempublicam against the republic, *dejecimusque*
and have dashed aside *mucrones eorum* their points
a jugulis vestris from your throats. 3. *Quæ* which
things *quoniam* since *illustrata sunt* they have been
revealed *in senatu* in the senate, *patefacta* made
manifest *comperta* and discovered *per me* through
me, *jam exponam* I will now explain them *vobis* to
you *breviter* briefly, *Quirites* Romans ; *ut* that *vos*
you *qui* who *ignoratis* are ignorant, *possitis* may be
able *scire* to know *ex actis* from what has been done
et both *quanta* how great [they were] *et* and *quam*
manifesta how manifest *et* and *qua ratione* in what

52

manner *investigata sint* they were investigated *et comprehensa* and grasped.

Principio in the first place, *ut* when *Catilina* Catiline *erupit* broke out *ex urbe* from the city *paucis ante diebus* a few days ago, *quum* when *reliquisset* he had left *Romæ* at Rome *socios* the associates *sui sceleris* of his wickedness, *duces acerrimos* the active leaders *hujusce nefarii belli* of this nefarious war, *semper vigilavi* I have always watched *et providi* and provided, *Quirites* Romans, *quemadmodum* how *possemus* we might *esse* be *salvi* safe *in tantis* amid such great *et* and *tam absconditis insidiis* such hidden plots.

II. *Nam* for *tum* at that time, *quum* when *ejiciebam* I was casting out *Catilinam* Catiline *ex urbe* from the city (*jam enim* for now *non vereor* I do not fear *invidiam* the odium *hujus verbi* of this word, *quum* seeing that *illa* that [odium] *est* is *magis* more *timenda* to be feared, *quod* that *exierit* he went forth *vivus* alive,) *sed* but *tum* then, *quum* when *volebam* I wished *illum* him *exterminari* to be cast out, *putabam* I thought *aut* either *reliquam manum* that the rest of the band *conjuratorum* of conspirators *exituram* would go forth *simul* with him *aut* or *eos* that those *qui* who *restitissent* should have remained, *fore* would be *infirmos* infirm *ac debiles* and weak *sine illo* without him. 4. *Atque* and *ego* I *ut* when *vidi* I saw *eos* that those *quos* whom *sciebam* I knew *esse inflammatos* to have been inflamed *maximo furore* with the greatest fury *et scelere* and wickedness, *esse* were *nobiscum* with us *et* and *remansisse* remained *Romæ* at Rome, *consumpsi* spent *omnes dies* all my days *noctesque* and nights *in eo* on this point *ut* that *sentirem* I might know *ac viderem* and see *quid* what *agerent* they were doing, *quid* what *molirentur* they were planning, *ut* that *quoniam* since *mea oratio* my speech *faceret* would create *minorem fidem* less belief *auribus vestris* in your ears, *propter* on account of *incredibilem magnitudinem* the incredible greatness *sceleris* of the wickedness, *ita compreҟenderem* I might so grasp *rem* the affair *ut* that *provideretis* you might provide *animis* in your minds *saluti vestræ* for your safety, *quum* when *videretis* you should see *oculis* with your eyes *maleficium ipsum* the wickedness itself. *Itaque* therefore *ut* when *comperi* I found out *legatos* that the ambassadors *Allobrogum* of the Allobroges *sollicitatos esse* had been solicited *a Publio Lentulo* by Publius Lentulus *causa* for the purpose *excitandi* of stirring up *belli transalpini* a transalpine war *et* and *Gallici tumultus* a tumult in Gaul, *eosque* and that they *esse missos* had been sent *in Galliam* into Gaul *ad suos cives* to their own countrymen *eodemque itinere* and on the same journey *cum literis* with letters *mandatisque* and instructions *ad Catilinam* to Catiline. *Vulturciumque* and that Vulturcius *adjunctum* was joined *comitem* as a companion *iis* to them, *atque* and *literas* that letters *datas esse* were given *huic* to him *ad Catilinam* to [carry to] Catiline; *putavi* I thought *facultatem* that the power *oblatam* was offered *mihi* to me, *ut* that *tota res* the whole affair (*quod* which *erat* was *difficillimum* most difficult, *quodque* and which *ego* I *semper optabam* always wished *a diis immortalibus* from the immortal gods) *deprehenderetur* might be detected *manifesto* clearly *non solum* not only *a me* by me *sed etiam* but also *a senatu* by the senate *et* and *a vobis* by you. 5. *Itaque* therefore *hesterno die* yesterday *vocavi* I summoned *ad me* to me *prætores* the prætors, *Lucium Flaccum* Lucius Flaccus *et* and *Caium Pomptinum* Caius Pomptinus, *viros* men *fortissimos* of the greatest courage *atque* and *amantissimos reipublicæ* most attached to the republic; *exposui* I explained to them *totam rem* the whole affair; *ostendi* I pointed out *quid* what *placeret* it seemed good *fieri* to be done. *Illi autem* but they, *qui* [men] who *sentire* ￭

54

omnia had all their sentiments *præclara* noble *atque egregia* and elevated *de republica* about the republic, *susceperunt* undertook *negotium* the business *sine recusatione* without hesitation *ac* and *sine ulla mora* without any delay, *et* and, *quum* when *advesperasceret* it was growing towards evening, *pervenerunt* arrived *occulte* secretly *ad pontem Mulvium* at the Mulvian bridge, *atque* and *ibi* there *fuerunt* were *in proximis villis* in the neighbouring villas *bipartito* in two parties *ita* so *ut* that *Tiberis* the Tiber *et pons* and the bridge *interesset* intervened *inter eos* between them. *Et ipsi autem* but themselves also *sine suspicione* without the suspicion *cujusquam* of anyone *eduxerunt* led out *eodem* to the same place *multos fortes viros* many brave men, *et ego* and I *miseram* had sent *cum gladiis* armed with swords *complures delectos adolescentes* several chosen young men *ex præfectura Reatina* from the prefecture of Reate, *quorum opera* whose service *assidue utor* I constantly use *in republica* in the state *præsidio* as a guard. 6. *Interim* meanwhile *tertia fere vigilia* about the third watch *exacta* having been completed, *quum* when *legati* the ambassadors *Allobrogum* of the Allobroges *magno comitatu* in a great company *jam inciperent* were already beginning *ingredi* to enter upon *pontem Milvium* the Milvian bridge *Vulturciusque* and Vulturcius *una* together with them, *impetus* an attack *fit* is made *in eos* upon them : *gladii* swords *educuntur* are drawn *et ab illis* both by them *et* and *a nostris* by our men. *Res* the matter *erat* was *nota* known *prætoribus solis* to the prætors alone ; *ignorabatur* it was not known *a cæteris* by the others.

III. *Tum* then *interventu* by the intervention *Pomptini* of Pomptinus *atque Flacci* and of Flaccus, *pugna* the fight, *quæ* which *erat commissa* had been begun, *sedatur* is appeased. *Litteræ quæcunque* whatever letters *erant* were *in eo comitatu* in that

55

company, *traduntur* are handed over *prœtoribus* to the prætors *integris signis* with their seals unbroken ; *ipsi* themselves *comprehensi* having been seized *deducuntur* are conducted *ad me* to me, *quum* when *jam dilucesceret* it was already dawning. *Atque* and *statim vocavi* I immediately summoned *ad me* to me *Cimbrum Gabinium* Cimber Gabinius *improbissimum machinatorem* the wicked contriver *horum omnium scelerum* of all these crimes, *suspicantem* suspecting *nihildum* nothing yet. *Deinde* after that *Publius Statilius* Publius Statilius *item* also *arcessitur* is sent for, *et post eum* and after him *Caius Cethegus* Caius Cethegus. *Lentulus autem* but Lentulus *venit* came *tardissime* very tardily, *quod* because (*credo* I believe) *vigilarat* he had sat up *proxima nocte* the night before *præter consuetudinem* beyond his custom *literis dandis* in dispatching letters. 7. *Quum vero* but when *placeret* it seemed good *summis* to the highest *ac clarissimis viris* and most noble men *hujus civitatis* of this city, *qui* who, *audita re* having heard of the matter, *convenerant* had come together *frequentes* in numbers *ad me* to my house *mane* in the morning, *literas* that the letters *aperiri* should be opened *a me* by me *priusquam* before that *deferri* they should be carried *ad senatum* to the senate, *ne* lest *tantus tumultus* so great a tumult *videretur* should seem *injectus* caused *civitati* to the city *a me* by me *temere* for nothing, *si* if *nihil* nothing *esset inventum* was found in them : *negavi* I denied *me* that I *facturum esse* would so act, *ut non deferrem* so as not to report *rem integram* the whole matter *de periculo publico* about a public peril *ad publicum consilium* to the public counsel. *Etenim* for also, *Quirites* Romans. *si* if *ea* those things, *quæ* which *erant delata* had been reported *ad me* to me, *non essent reperta* had not been found out [to be true], *tamen* yet *ego* I *non arbitrabar* did not think *nimiam diligentiam* that too great diligence *esse pertimescendam* was to be feared *mihi* by me *is tantis periculis* amid such great dangers *reipublicæ* of the republic. *Coegi* I assembled *senatum frequentem* a full senate, *ut* as *vidistis* you have seen, *celeriter* speedily. 8. *Atque* and *interim* meanwhile, *admonitu* by the advice *Allobrogum* of the Allobroges *statim misi* I immediately sent *Caium Sulpicium* Caius Sulpicius *prætorem* the prætor *fortem virum* a brave man, *qui efferret* to bring forth *ex ædibus* out of the house *Cethegi* of Cethegus *si quid telorum* whatever weapons *esset* might be [found there] ; *ex quibus* out of which *ille* he *extulit* brought forth *maximum numerum* a very great number *sicarum* of daggers *et gladiorum* and of swords.

IV. *Introduxi* I introduced *Vulturcium* Vulturcius *sine Gallis* without the Gauls : *dedi* I gave *ei* to him *fidem publicam* the public pledge [of safety] *jussu* by command *senatus* of the senate : *hortatus sum* I exhorted him *ut indicaret* to tell *sine metu* without fear *ea* those things *quæ* which *sciret* he knew. *Tum* then *ille* he, *quum* when *vix se recreasset* he had hardly recovered *se* himself *ex magno timore* from his great fear, *dixit* said, *se* that he *habere* had *mandata* instructions *et literas* and letters *a Publio Lentulo* from Publius Lentulus *ad Catilinam* to Catiline, *ut* that *uteretur* he should use *præsidio* the protection *servorum* of the slaves *et accederet* and approach *quamprimum* as soon as possible *cum exercitu* with his army *ad urbem* to the city : *id autem* and that *eo consilio* with this design *ut* that, *quum* when *incendissent* they should have fired *urbem* the city *omnibus ex partibus* in every part *fecissentque* and should have made *infinitam cædem* an immense slaughter *civium* of the citizens, *ille* he *esset* might be *præsto* at hand, *qui* who *et* both *exciperet* might cut off *fugientes* the fugitives *et* and *conjungeret* join *se* himself *cum his urbanis ducibus* with these leaders in the city. 9. *Galli autem* but the Gauls *introducti* having been introduced *dixerunt* said *jusjurandum*

57

that an oath *et* and *literas* letters *datas esse* had been given *sibi* to them *a Publio Lentulo* by Publius Lentulus, *Cethego* Cethegus, *Statilio* and Statilius *ad* *suam gentem* to their own people, *atque* and *præscriptum esse* orders had been given *sibi* to them *ab his* by these *et* and *Lucio Cassio* by Lucius Cassius *ita* to this effect, *ut* that *mitterent* they should send *equitatum* cavalry *in Italiam* into Italy *quamprimum* as soon as possible, *pedestres copias* that foot-soldiers *non defuturas* would not be wanting *sibi* to them : *Lentulum autem* but that Lentulus *confirmasse · sibi* had settled it in his own mind *ex fatis Sibyllinis* from the Sibylline prophecies *responsisque* and the answers *haruspicum* of the haruspices *se* that he *esse* was *tertium illum Cornelium* that third Cornelius, *ad quem* to whom *necesse esset* it was fated *regnum* that the rule *atque imperium* and empire *hujus urbis* of this city *pervenire* should come ; *fuisse* that there had been *Cinnam* Cinna *et Sullam* and Sulla *ante se* before him ; *eundemque* and that the same man *dixisse* had said *hunc annum* that this year *esse* was *fatalem* destined *ad interitum* for the destruction *hujus urbis* of this city *atque imperii* and empire, *qui* which *esset* was *decimus annus* the tenth year *post absolutionem* since the acquittal *virginum* of the virgins, *vicesimus autem* but the twentieth *post incensionem* since the burning *Capitolii* of the Capitol. 10. *Dixerunt autem* but they said *fuisse* that there had been *Cethego* to Cethegus *hanc controversiam* this controversy *cum cæteris* with the others, *quod* that *quum* whereas *placeret* it seemed good *Lentulo* to Lentulus *et aliis* and to others *cædem* that the slaughter *fieri* should be made *atque* and *urbem* the city *incendi* be fired *Saturnalibus* on the Saturnalia *id* that *videretur* seemed *longum* tedious *Cethego* to Cethegus.

V. *Ac* and *ne sit* that it may not be *longum* long, *Quirites* Romans, *jussimus* we ordered *tabellas* writings *proferri* to be put forwards *quæ* which *dixe*

buntur were said *datæ* to have been given *a quoque* by
each. *Primum* first *ostendimus* we showed *signum*
the seal *Cethego* to Cethegus ; *cognovit* he knew it.
Nos we *incidimus* cut *linum* the thread : *legimus* we
read it. *Erat scriptum* it was written *manu* by the
hand *ipsius* of himself *senatui* to the senate *et populo*
and people *Allobrogum* of the Allobroges, *sese* that he
facturum esse would do *quæ* what *confirmasset* he had
guaranteed *legatis eorum* to their ambassadors : *orare*
that he entreated *ut* that *item illi* they also *facerent*
would do *quæ* what *legati eorum* their ambassadors
præcepissent sibi had instructed them to do. *Tum*
then *Cethegus* Cethegus, *qui* who *paullo ante* a little
before *tamen* nevertheless *respondisset* had answered
dixissetque and had said *aliquid* something *de gladiis*
about the swords *ac sicis* and daggers *quæ* which *de-
prehensæ erant* had been found *apud ipsum* in his
house, *dixissetque* and had said *se* that he *semper
fuisse* had always been *studiosum* fond *bonorum fer-
ramentorum* of good steel weapons, *debilitatus* being
weakened *atque abjectus* and cast down *recitatis literis*
when the letters were read, *convictus* convicted *conscientia* by his conscience, *repente* suddenly *conticuit*
was silent. *Statilius* Statilius *introductus est* was introduced : *cognovit* he knew *et signum* both the seal
et and *manum suam* his hand [-writing]. *Tabellæ* the
tablets *recitatæ sunt* were read *fore* almost *in eandem
sententiam* to the same import : *confessus est* he confessed. *Tum ostendi* I then showed *tabellas* the tablets *Lentulo* to Lentulus *et quæsivi* and asked *cog-
nosceretne* whether he recognized *signum* the seal.
Annuit he assented. "*Est vero* it is indeed," *inquam*
I say, "*signum notum* a well-known seal, *imago* the
likeness *avi tui* of your grandfather, *clarissimi viri* a
most illustrious man, *qui* who *unice amavit* singu-
larly loved *patriam* his country *et* and *cives suos* his
countrymen, *quæ quidem* which indeed *etiam muta*
even without speaking *debuit revocare* ought to have

recalled *te* you *a tanto scelere* from such great wic
edness. 11. *Literæ* the letters *ad senatum* to the
senate *populumque* and people *Allobrogum* of the
Allobroges *leguntur* are read *eadem ratione* in the
same manner: *si* if *vellet* he wished *dicere* to say
quid any thing *de his rebus* about these matters, *feci*
potestatem I gave him leave [to say it]. *Atque ille*
and he *primo quidem* at first indeed *negavit* denied;
aliquanto autem but a little *post* afterwards, *toto in-*
dicio the whole information *exposito jam* having been
now set forth *atque edito* and made public, *surrexit*
he rose; *quæsivit* he asked *a Gallis* from the Gauls
quid sibi esset what he had to do *cum iis* with them;
quamobrem why *venissent* they had come *domum*
suam to his house; *itemque* and the same *a Vulturcio*
from Vulturcius. *Qui who quum* when *respondissent*
[they] had replied *breviter* briefly *constanterque* and
steadily *per quem* by whose mediation *quotiesque* and
how often *venissent* they had come *ad eum* to him
quæsissentque and had asked *ab eo* from him *essetne*
loquutus whether he had spoken *nihil* nothing *secum*
with them *de fatis Sibyllinis* about the Sybilline prophecies; *tum* then *ille* he *subito* suddenly *demens*
mad *scelere* with crime *ostendit* showed *quanta* how
great *esset* was *vis* the power *conscientiæ* of conscience. *Nam* for, *quum* whereas *posset* he was able
infitiari to deny *id* that, *repente* on a sudden *confessus*
est he confessed it *præter opinionem* contrary to the
opinion *omnium* of all: *ita* thus *non modo* not only
ingenium illud that talent *et exercitatio* and practice
dicendi in speaking *qua* in which *semper valuit* he
was always strong *sed* but *etiam* also *propter vim* by
the force *scelerts* of his crime *manifesti* manifest
atque deprehensi and detected, *impudentia* his ef-
frontery *qua* in which *superabat* he surpassed *omnes*
all men *improbitasque* and his villainy *defecit eum*
failed him.

12. *Vulturcius vero* but Vulturcius *subito* on a sud

den *jussit* ordered *literas* letters *proferri* to be produced *atque* and *aperiri* to be opened, *quas* which *dicebat* he said *datas esse* had been given *sibi* to him a *Lentulo* by Lentulus *ad Catilinam* to [give to] Catiline. *Atque* and *ibi* upon that *Lentulus* Lentulus *perturbatus* agitated *vehementissime* most violently, *tamen* nevertheless *cognovit* recognized *et* both *signum suum* his seal *et manum* and hand[writing]. *Erant autem scriptæ* but they were written *sine nomine* without a name *sed* but *ita* to this effect: "*Cognosces* you will learn *qui* who *sim* I am *ex eo* from him *quem* whom *misi* I have sent *ad te* to you. *Cura* take care *ut sis* to be *vir* a man, *et cogita* and consider *in quem locum* into what a position *progressus sis* you have advanced, *et vide* and see *quid* what *jam* now *sit necesse* is necessary *tibi* for you. *Cura* take care *ut adjungas* to attach *tibi* to you *auxilia* the aid *omnium* of all, *etiam* even *infimorum* of the lowest." *Deinde* then *Gabinius* Gabinius *introductus* having been introduced, *quum* when *primo* at first *cœpisset* he had begun *respondere* to answer *impudenter* impudently, *ad extremum* at last *negavit* denied *nihil* nothing *ex iis* of those matters *quæ* which *Galli* the Gauls *insimulabant* charged against him. 13. *Ac* and *mihi quidem* to me indeed, *Quirites* Romans, *quum* not only *illa* did these *visa sunt* seem *certissima argumenta* the most certain proofs *atque indicia* and signs *sceleris* of guilt, *tabellæ* the tablets, *signa* the seals, *manus* the hand[writing], *denique* lastly *confessio* the confession *uniuscujusque* of each one, *tum* but also *illa* these *multo certiora* much more certain, *color* their [pale] colour, *oculi* their [downcast] eyes, *vultus* their look, *taciturnitas* their silence. *Obstupuerant enim* for they had become stupefied *sic* to such a degree, *intuebantur* they looked on *terram* the ground *sic* in such a manner, *sic adspiciebant* they so looked *inter se* at one another *nonnunquam* at times *tim* privately *ut* that *viderentur* they seemed *non*

61

jam not now *judicari* to be judged *sed* but *ipsi* them-selves *judicare* to judge *se* themselves.

VI. *Indiciis* the proofs *expositis* having been set forth *atque editis* and made public, *Quirites* Romans, *consului* I consulted *senatum* the senate *quid* what *placeret* it should seem good *fieri* to be done *de summa republica* about the republic in general. *Acerrimæ* most energetic *ac fortissimæ sententiæ* and bold opinions *dictæ sunt* were uttered *a principibus* by the leading men, *quas* which *senatus* the senate *consequutus est* followed *sine ulla varietate* without any variation. *Et* and *quoniam* since *senatus consultum* the decree of the senate *est* is *nondum perscriptum* not yet written out *exponam* I will explain *vobis* to you, *Quirites* Romans, *ex memoria* from memory, *quid* what *senatus* the senate *censuerit* decreed. 14. *Primum* first *gratiæ* thanks *aguntur* are given *mihi* to me *amplissimis verbis* in the most ample [form of] words, *quod* because *mea virtute* by my valour, *consilio* prudence *providentia* and forethought *respublica* the republic *liberata sit* has been freed *maximis periculis* from the greatest dangers : *deinde* then *Lucius Flaccus* Lucius Flaccus *et* and *Caius Pomptinus* Caius Pomptinus, *prætores* the prætors, *laudantur* are praised *merito* deservedly *ac jure* and justly *quod* because *usus essem* I had used *eorum forti* their bold *fidelique opera* and faithful service : *atque* and *laus* praise *etiam* also *impertitur* is bestowed *viro forti* on that brave man *collegæ meo* my colleague, *quod* because *removisset* he had removed *a suis consiliis* from his counsels *et reipublicæ* and [the counsels] of the republic *eos* those *qui* who *fuissent* had been *participes* partakers *hujus conjurationis* of this conspiracy. *Atque* and *censuerunt* they decreed *ita* to this effect *ut* that *Publius Lentulus* Publius Lentulus, *quum* when *abdicasset se* he had abdicated *prætura* the prætorship, *tum traderetur* should then be delivered *in custodiam* into custody

itemque and also *ut* that *Caius Cethegus* Caius Cethegus, *Lucius Statilius* Lucius Statilius, *Publius
Gabinius* and Publius Gabinius, *qui omnes* all of
whom *erant* were *præsentes* present, *traderentur*
should be handed over *in custodiam* into custody :
atque and *hoc idem* this same [sentence] *decretum est*
was decreed *in Lucium Cassium* against Lucius Cassius, *qui* who *depoposcerat* had demanded *sibi* for
himself *procurationem* the charge *incendendæ urbis* of
burning the city; *in Marcum Ceparium* against
Marcus Ceparius, *cui* to whom *indicatum erat* it had
been stated *Apuliam* that Apulia *attributam esse* was
assigned *ad pastores sollicitandos* to stir up the shep-
herds; *in Publium Furium* against Publius Furius,
qui who *est* is *ex his colonis* [one] of those colonists
quos whom *Lucius Sulla* Lucius Sulla *deduxit* conducted *Fæsulas* to Fæsulæ; *in Quintum Manlium
Chilonem* against Quintus Manlius Chilo, *qui* who
semper versatus erat had always been engaged *una*
together *cum hoc Furio* with this Furius *in hac sol-
licitatione* in this solicitation *Allobrogum* of the Allobroges ; *in Publium Umbrenum* against Publius
Umbrenus, *libertinum hominem* a freedman, *a quo* by
whom *constabat* it was established *Gallos* that the
Gauls *primum perductos esse* were first brought *ad
Gabinium* to Gabinius.

Atque and *senatus* the senate *usus est* used *ea lenitate* such lenity, *Quirites* Romans, *ut* that *ex tanto
conjuratione* out of so great a conspiracy *tantaque vi*
and such a force *ac multitudine* and number *hostium
domesticorum* of domestic enemies, *republica* the
state *conservata* having been preserved *pœna* by the
punishment *novem hominum* of nine men *perditissimorum* the most abandoned, *arbitrabatur* he thought
mentes that the minds *reliquorum* of the rest, *posse*
might *sanari* be cured. 15. *Atque* and *etiam* moreover *supplicatio* thanksgiving *decreta est* was decreed
meo nomine in my name *diis imm*   ·n-

mortal gods *pro singulari eorum merito* for their singular service, *Quirites* Romans; *quod* which *contigit primum* has first happened *mihi* to me *togato* a civilian *post hanc urbem conditam* since this city was built; *et* and *decreta est* it was decreed *his verbis* in these words, "*quod* because *liberassem* I had freed *urbem* the city *incendiis* from flames, *cives* the citizens *cæde* from slaughter, *Italiam* Italy *bello* from war." *Quæ supplicatio* which thanksgiving *si* if *conferatur* it be compared *cum cæteris* with the others, *Quirites* Romans, *hoc interest* there is this difference *quod* that *cæteræ* the others [were appointed] *republica bene gesta* when the republic had been successfully administered, *hæc una* this one alone *conservata* because it was saved. *Atque* and *illud* that *quod* which *fuit* was *faciendum* necessary to be done *primum* the first thing, *factum est* has been done *atque transactum* and finished. *Nam* for *Publius Lentulus* Publius Lentulus, *quanquam* although, *indiciis patefactis* when the proofs were exhibited *et* and *confessionibus suis* by his own confession *amiserat* he had lost *judicio* by the judgment *senatus* of the senate *jus* the right *non modo* not only *prætoris* of the prætor *verum etiam* but also *civis* of a citizen, *tamen* yet *abdicavit se* withdrew himself *magistratu* from the magistracy: *ut* so that *nos* we *liberaremur* might be freed *in puniendo* in punishing *Publio Lentulo* Publius Lentulus *privato* a private man *ea religione* from that religious scruple *quæ* which *non fuerat* had not existed *Caio Mario* to Caius Marius *clarissimo viro* a most illustrious man, *quominus occideret* to prevent his slaying *Caium Glauciam* Caius Glaucias, *prætorem* the prætor, *de quo* about whom *nominatim* by name *nihil* nothing *decretum erat* had been decreed.

VII. 16. *Nunc* now, *Quirites* Romans, *quoniam* since *tenetis* you hold *nefarios duces* the wicked leaders *sceleratissimi* of this most criminal *periculosissimique belli* and most dangerous war *cum captos* already captured *et comprehensos* and in custody, *debetis existimare* you must think *omnes copias* that all the forces *Catilinæ* of Catiline, *omnes spes* that all his hopes *atque opes* and means *concidisse* have fallen, *his periculis* these dangers *urbis* of the city *depulsis* having been repelled. *Quem quidem* whom indeed *quum* when *pellebam* I was driving *ex urbe* out of the city, *providebam* I foresaw *hoc* this *animo* in my mind, *Quirites* Romans, *remoto Catilina* [that,] if Catiline was removed *nec somnum* neither the sleep *Publii Lentuli* of Publius Lentulus, *nec* nor *adipem* the fat *Lucii Cassii* of Lucius Cassius, *nec* nor *furio-sam temeritatem* the furious rashness *Cethegi* of Ce-thegus *esse* was *pertimescendam* alarming *mihi* for me. *Ille* he *unus* alone *ex his omnibus* of all these *erat* was *timendus* to be feared *mihi* by me ; *sed* but *tam diu* [only] so long, *dum* whilst *continebatur* he was contained *mœnibus* within the walls *urbis* of the city. *Norat* he knew *omnia* all things, *tenebat* he possessed *aditus* the approaches *omnium* of all : *po-terat* he was able, *audebat* and he dared *appellare* to address, *tentare* to tempt, *sollicitare* and to solicit [people] : *erat* there was *ei* in him *consilium* con-trivance *aptum* suited *ad facinus* to commit crime : *consilio autem* but to his skill in contriving *neque lingua* neither tongue *neque manus* nor hand *deerat* was wanting. *Jam habebat* he already had *certos homines* trusty men *delectos* chosen *ac descriptos* and arranged *ad ceteras res conficiendas* to execute the other matters. *Neque vero* but neither, *quum* when *mandaverat* he had commanded *aliquid* any thing, *putabat* did he think it *confectum* done : *erat* there was *nihil* nothing, *quod* which *ipse* himself *non obiret* did not attend to, *occurreret* go to meet *vigilaret* sit up late [about,] *laboraret* and toil [at] : *poterat* he was able *ferre* to bear *frigus* cold, *sitim* thirst, *famem* and hunger. 17. *Nisi* unless *ego* I *compulissem* had driven *ex domesticis insidiis* from domestic plots in

65

tatrocinium castrense to the brigandage of a camp, *hunc hominem* this man *tam acrem* so active, *tam paratum* so prompt, *tam audacem* so bold, *tam callidum* so cunning, *tam vigilantem* so watchful *in scelere* in crime, *tam diligentem* so diligent *in perditis rebus* in desperate circumstances, (*dicam* I will speak *id* that *quod* which *sentio* I think, *Quirites* Romans) *non facile depulissem* I should not easily have turned aside *hanc molem* this weight *belli* of war *tantam* so great *a cervicibus vestris* from your shoulders. *Ille* he *non constituisset* would not have fixed on *Saturnalia* the Saturnalia *nobis* for us, *neque* nor *denuntiasset* have declared *tanto ante* so long before *diem* the day *exitii* of destruction *et fati* and of fate *reipublicæ* for the republic, *neque* nor *commisisset* have so acted, *ut* that *signum* his seal, *ut* that *literæ suæ* his letters, *testes* the witnesses, *denique* in short, *manifesti sceleris* of his manifest guilt *deprehenderentur* should be taken. *Quæ* which things *sic gesta sunt* have been so done *nunc* now *illo absente* in his absence, *ut* that *nullum furtum* no theft *in privata domo* in a private house *unquam* ever *sit inventum* has been found out *tam palam* so openly, *quam* as *hæc tanta conjuratio* this so great conspiracy *in rempublicam* against the republic *manifesto* manifestly *inventa est* has been found out *atque deprehensa* and detected. *Quod si* but if *Catilina* Catiline *remansisset* had remained *in urbe* in the city *ad hanc diem* to this day *quanquam* although *occurri* I met *atque obstiti* and opposed *omnibus ejus consiliis* all his designs *quoad* as long as *fuit* he was [here], *tamen* yet, *ut dicam* to speak *levissime* the most lightly, *dimicandum nobis fuisset* we should have had to fight *cum illo* with him *neque* nor *nos unquam liberassemus* should we ever have freed *rempublicam* the state *tantis periculis* from such great dangers, *dum* whilst *ille hostis* that enemy *fuisset* was *in urbe* in the city.

tanta pace with so much quiet, *tanto otio* with so much ease, *tanto silentio* and so much silence.

VIII. 18. *Quanquam* although *hæc omnia* all these things, *Quirites* Romans, *administrata sunt* have been managed *a me* by me *ita* in such a way *ut* that *videantur* they seem *et gesta esse* both to have been done *et provisa* and provided *nutu* at the beck *atque consilio* and by the wisdom *deorum immortalium* of the immortal gods, *quumque* and not only *possumus* can we *consequi* obtain *id* that *conjectura* by conjecture, *quod* because *gubernatio* the government *tantarum rerum* of such great affairs *vix* scarcely *videtur* seems *esse* to be *humani consilii* a matter of human wisdom, *tum vero* but also *tulerunt* they have brought *opem* aid *et auxilium* and help *nobis* to us *his temporibus* in these times *ita præsentes* so immediate *ut* that *possemus* we might *pæne* almost *videre* see *eos* them *oculis* with our eyes, *Nam* for, *ut omittam* to omit *illa* these things, *faces* torches *visas* seen *ab occidente* from the west *nocturno tempore* in the night time *ardoremque* and the heat *cœli* of the sky, *ut* as also *jactus* the launchings *fulminum* of thunderbolts, *ut* as *motus terræ* earthquakes, *ut* as *cætera* the other things, *quæ* which *facta sunt* have taken place *tam multa* in such great numbers, *nobis consulibus* during our consulship, *ut* that *dii immortales* the immortal gods *viderentur* seemed *canere* to foretell *hæc* these things *quæ* which *nunc fiunt* are now happening; *hoc* this *certe* at all events, *Quirites* Romans, *quod* which *dicturus sum* I am about to say, *est* is *neque* neither *prætermittendum* to be passed over *neque* nor *relinquendum* omitted. 19. *Nam* for *profecto* no doubt *tenetis* ye keep it *memoria* in your recollection, *complures turr x* that several towers *in Capitolio* in the Capitol *percussas esse* were struck *de cœlo* from heaven, *Cotta et Torquato consulibus* in the consulship of Cotta and Torquatus, *quum* when *et* both *simulacra* the images *deorum immortalium* of the immortal gods *depulsa sunt* were struck out of their places *et statuæ* and the statues *veterum hominum* of former men *dejectæ* thrown down, *et æra* and the brasses *legum* of the laws *liquefacta* were melted; *etiam* and also *ille Romulus* the great Romulus, *qui* who *condidit* built *hanc urbem* this city, *tactus est* was touched; *quem* whom *meministis* you remember *fuisse* to have been *in Capitolio* in the capitol *parvum* a little boy *inauratum* gilt *atque lactentem* and sucking, *inhiantem* opening his mouth *uberibus lupinis* for the teats of the she-wolf. *Quo quidem tempore* at which time indeed, *quum* when *haruspices* the haruspices *convenissent* had met together *ex tota Etruria* out of all Etruria, *dixerunt* they said *cædes* that slaughter *atque incendia* and flames *et interitum* and the destruction *legum* of the laws *et* and *civile* that civil *ac domesticum bellum* and domestic war *et occasum* and the fall *totius urbis* of the whole city *atque imperii* and empire *appropinquare* were approaching, *nisi* unless *dii immortales* the immortal gods *placati* appeased *omni ratione* in every possible manner, *prope flexissent* had almost bent *fata ipsa* the fates themselves *suo numine* by their influence. 20. *Itaque* therefore *responsis illorum* by their answers *tunc* at that time *et* both *ludi* games *facti sunt* were celebrated *decem per dies* during ten days, *neque* nor *res ulla* was any thing *prætermissa est* omitted, *quæ* which *pertineret* related *ad placandum deos* to appeasing the gods; *iidemque* and those same [haruspices] *jusserunt* ordered us *facere* to make *majus simulacrum* a greater image *Jovis* of Jupiter *et* and *collocare* to place it *in excelso* on high *et* and *convertere* turn it *ad orientem* towards the east, *contra atque* contrary to what *fuerat* it had been *ante* before, *ac* and *dixerunt* they said *se* that they *sperare* hoped, *si* that if *illud signum* that statue, *quod* which *videtis* you see, *conspiceret* looked towards *ortum* the

rising *solis* of the sun *et forum* and the forum *curi-
amque* and the senate house, *fore* it would come to
pass *ut* that *ea consilia* those designs *quæ* which *inita
essent* were entered upon *clam* secretly *contra salutem* against the welfare *urbis* of the city *atque imperii*
and the empire, *illustrarentur* would be brought to
light *ut* so that *possent* they might *perspici* be seen
through *a senatu* by the senate *populoque Romano*
and the Roman people. *Atque* and *consules illi* th ese
consuls *locaverunt* let out *illud* it *collocandum ita* to
be so placed : *sed* but *tanta* so great *fuit* was *tarditas*
the slowness *operis* of the work *ut* that *collocaretur* it
was placed *neque* neither *a superioribus consulibus* by
the former consuls *neque* nor *a nobis* by us *ante ho-
diernum diem* before this day.

IX. 21. *Hic* here, *Quirites* Romans, *quis* who *potest* can *esse* be *tam aversus* so averse *a vero* from the
truth, *tam præceps* so headstrong, *tam captus* so
enslaved *mente* in mind, *qui neget* as to deny *hæc
omnia* that all these things *quæ* which *videmus* we
see *præcipueque* and especially *hanc urbem* this city
administrari are regulated *nutu* by the will *atque
potestate* and power *deorum immortalium* of the immortal gods ? *Etenim* for indeed *quum* when *responsum esset* it had been answered *ita* to this effect
cædes that slaughter *incendia* flames, *interitumque* and
the destruction *reipublicæ* of the republic, *comparari*
were being prepared, *et ea* and those things *a perditis civibus* by abandoned citizens, *quæ* which *tum* then
videbantur seemed *nonnullis* to some *incredibilia* incredible *propter* on account of *magnitudinem* the
greatness *scelerum* of the crimes, *ea* those *sensistis* you
have seen *non modo* not only *cogitata esse* to have
been meditated *a nefariis civibus* by wicked citizens,
verum but *etiam* also *suscepta* undertaken. *Nonne
vero est* but is not *illud* this *ita præsens* so present *ut*
that *videatur* it seems *factum esse* to have happened
nutu by the will *Jovis* of Jupiter *Optimi Maximi*

Good and Great, *ut* that, *quum* when *hodierno die* this day *et* both *conjurati* the conspirators *et eorum indices* and their informers *ducerentur* were being led *in ædem* into the temple *Concordiæ* of Concord, *signum* the statue *statueretur* was being set up *eo ipso tempore* at that very time? *Quo collocato* which having been placed *atque converso* and turned *ad vos* to you *senatumque* and the senate, *et senatus* both the senate *et vos* and you *vidistis* saw *omnia* all [the plans] *quæ* which *erant cogitata* had been thought of *contra salutem* against the safety *omnium* of all *illustrata* brought to light *et patefacta* and revealed. 22. *Quo* whereby *etiam* also *isti* those men *sunt* are *digni* worthy of *majore odio* greater hatred *supplicioque* and punishment, *qui* who *conati sunt* have endeavoured *inferre* to apply *funestos* fatal *ac* and *nefarios ignes* unholy flames *non solum* not only *vestris domiciliis* · to your homes *atque tectis* and roofs, *sed etiam* but also *templis* to the temples *atque delubris* and shrines *deorum* of the gods. *Quibus* to whom *si* if *ego dicam* I say *me* that I *restitisse* made resistance, *sumam* I should assume *nimium* too much *mihi* to myself *et ana non sim* should not be *ferendus* to be borne by you. *Ille* it was he—*ille Jupiter* that Jupiter *restitit* who resisted; *ille* he *voluit* wished *Capitolium* the Capitol, *ille* he *hæc templa* these temples, *ille* he *hanc urbem* this city, *ille* he *vos omnes* all of you *esse* to be *salvos* safe. *Ego* I, *Quirites* O Romans, *suscepi* have received *hanc mentem* this state of mind, *voluntatemque* and will *diis immortalibus ducibus* with the immortal gods to guide me, *atque* and *perveni* arrived *ad hæc indicia* at these proofs *tanta* so great. *Jam vero* but now *illa sollicitatio* that solicitation *Allobrogum* of the Allobroges, *a Lentulo* by Lentulus *cæterisque domesticis hostibus* and our other domestic enemies, *tanta res* so great a matter [would never have been] *credita* entrusted *tam dementer* so foolishly *et ignotis* to men both unknown *et barbaris* and

barbarians, *litteræque* and those letters *nunquam*
never *essent commissæ* would have been committed
profecto assuredly *nisi* unless *consilium* wisdom
créptum esset had been taken away *a diis immortali-*
bus by the immortal gods *huic tantæ audaciæ* from
this great act of audacity. *Quid vero* but what?
ut that *homines Galli* men of Gaul *ex civitate* from
a city *male pacata* imperfectly pacificated, *quæ* which
una gens [is] the only nation *restat* [that] remains,
quæ which *videatur* seems *et* both *posse* to be able
et and *non nolle* not to be unwilling *facere bellum* to
make war *populo Romano* on the Roman people,
negligerent should neglect *spem* the hope *imperii* of
empire *et* and *rerum amplissimarum* of the greatest
prosperity *oblatam* offered *sibi* to them *ultro* gratu-
itously *a patriciis hominibus* by men who are patricians, *anteponerentque* and prefer *vestram salutem*
your safety *suis opibus* to their own power, *non pu-*
tatis do you not think *id* that that *factum esse* was
brought to pass *divinitus* from heaven? *præsertim*
especially *qui* [since they were men] who *potuerunt*
were able *superare* to overcome *nos* us *non pugnando*
not by fighting *sed* but *tacendo* by keeping silence.
   X. 23. *Quamobrem* wherefore, *Quirites* Romans,
quoniam since *supplicatio* a thanksgiving *decreta est*
has been decreed *ad omnia pulvinaria* at all the
shrines, *celebratote* celebrate *illos dies* those days
cum conjugibus vestris with your wives *ac liberis* and
children. *Nam* for *multi honores* many honours *sæpe*
habiti sunt have been often paid *diis immortalibus* to
the immortal gods *justi* just *ac debiti* and due *sed*
but *profecto* without doubt *nunquam* never *justiores*
more just. *Erepti enim estis* for you have been
rescued *ex crudelissimo* from a most cruel *ac miser-*
rimo interitu and most miserable death, *et* and
erepti having been rescued *sine cæde* without slaughter, *sine sanguine* without blood, *sine exercitu*
without an army, *sine dimicatione* without fighting

togati you civilians *vicistis* have conquered, *me uno* me alone *togato* a civilian *duce* being your leader *et imperatore* and commander in chief. 24. *Etenim* for moreover *recordamini* call to mind, *Quirites* Romans, *omnes civiles dissentiones* all our civil dissensions, *neque solum* and not only *eas* those *quas* which *audistis* you have heard, *sed* but *et has* these also *quas* which *vosmet ipsi* you yourselves *meministis* remember *et vidistis* and have seen. *Lucius Sulla* Lucius Sulla *oppressit* crushed *Publium Sulpicium* Publius Sulpicius: *ejecit* he cast out *ex urbe* from the city *Caium Marium* Caius Marius, *custodem* the guardian *hujus urbis* of this city, *multosque fortes viros* and many brave men *partim ejecit* he partly cast out *ex urbe* from the city, *partim* partly *interemit* he put to death. *Cneius Octavius* Cneius Octavius *consul* the consul *expulit* expelled *collegam suum* his colleague *armis* by arms *ex urbe* from the city: *omnis hic locus* all this place *redundavit* overflowed *acervis* with heaps *corporum* of bodies *et sanguine* and with the blood *civium* of the citizens. *Postea* afterwards *Cinna* Cinna *cum Mario* with Marius *superavit* had the upper hand; *tum vero* but then *clarissimis viris* the most illustrious men *interfectis* having been put to death *lumina* the lights *civitatis* of the state *extincta sunt* were extinguished. *Sulla* Sulla *postea* afterwards *ultus est* avenged *crudelitatem* the cruelty *hujus victoriæ* of this victory, *nec quidem* nor indeed *est opus* is it needful *dici* to be said, *quanta diminutione* with what a diminution *civium* of the citizens, *et* and *quanta calamitate* with what calamity *reipublicæ* of the republic *Marcus Lepidus* Marcus Lepidus *dissensit* differed *a clarissimo* from that illustrious *et fortissimo viro* and brave man *Quinto Catulo* Quintus Catulus: *ipsius interitus* his death *attulit* brought *non tam* not so much *luctum* mourning *reipublicæ* to the republic *quam* as *cæterorum* [the death] of the

others. **25.** *Atque* and *illæ dissensiones* those dissensions, *Quirites* Romans, *erant* were *hujusmodi* of
such kind, *quæ* which *pertinerent* tended *non* not
ad delendam to destroy *sed* but *ad commutandam
rempublicam* to change [the constitution] of the state.
Illi those men *voluerunt* wished *non* not *esse* that
there should be *nullam rempublicam* no republic at
all, *sed* but *se* that they *esse* might be *principes* leaders
in ea in that state *quæ* which *esset* might be in existence, *neque* and not *hanc urbem* that this city
conflagrare should be in flames, *sed* but *se* that they
florere might thrive *in hac urbe* in this city. *Atque
tamen* and yet *omnes illæ dissensiones* all those dissensions, *quarum* of which *nulla* none *quæsivit*
sought *exitium* the destruction *reipublicæ* of the
state, *fuerunt* were *ejusmodi* of such sort *ut* that *di-
judicatæ sint* they were decided *non* not *reconcilia-
tione* by the reestablishment *concordiæ* of concord,
sed but *internecione* by internecine wars *civium* of
the citizens. *In hoc autem bello* but in this war
uno alone *maximo* the greatest *crudelissimoque* and
most cruel *post memoriam* since the memory *hominum* of men, *quale bellum* such a war as *nulla bar-
baria* no barbarous nation *unquam gessit* ever carried
on *cum sua gente* with its people, *quo in bello* in
which war *hæc lex* this law *fuit constituta* was laid
down *a Lentulo* by Lentulus, *Catilina* Catiline, *Cassio* Cassius, *Cethego* and Cethegus, *ut* that *omnes*
all *qui* who *possent* could *esse* be *salvi* safe *salva
urbe* with the city safe too, *ducerentur* should be
reckoned *in numero* in the number *hostium* of enemies, *gessi me* I bore myself, *Quirites* Romans, *ita*
in such wise, *ut* that *omnes* you all *conservaremini*
should be kept *salvi* safe; *et* and *quum* although
hostes vestri your enemies *putassent* had thought
tantum that [only] so large a part *civium* of the
citizens *superfuturum* would survive *quantum*

73

restitisset had resisted *infinitæ cædi* the unbounded massacre, *tantum autem* and [only] so much *urbis* of the city *quantum* as *flamma* the flame *non pctuisset* should not have been able *obire* to compass, *servavi* I preserved *et urbem* both the city *et cives* and the citizens *integros* sound *incolumesque* and safe.

XI. 26. *Quibus pro rebus* for which things *tantis* so great, *Quirites* Romans, *ego* I *postulo* demand *a vobis* from you *nullum præmium* no reward *virtutis* of merit, *nullum insigne* no mark *honoris* of honour, *nullum monumentum* no monument *laudis* of praise, *præterquam* otherwise than *sempiternam memoriam* the lasting memory *hujus diei* of this day. *Ego* I *volo* wish *omnes triumphos meos* all my triumphs, *omnia ornamenta* all my ornaments *honoris* of honour, *monumenta* monuments *gloriæ* of glory, *insignia* marks *laudis* of praise, *condi* to be laid up *et collocari* and placed *in animis vestris* in your minds. *Nihil* nothing *mutum* mute, *nihil* nothing *tacitum* silent *potest* can *delectare* delight *me* me, *nihil* nothing *denique* in short *hujusmodi* of this sort, *quod* which *etiam* even *minus digni* less worthy men *possint* are able *assequi* to attain to. *Vostræ res* my achievements, *Quirites* Romans, *alentur* will be cherished *memoria vestra* in your memory, *crescent* will grow *sermonibus* by your talk, *inveterascent* will become rooted, *et corroborabuntur* and will be confirmed *monumentis* by the monuments *literarum* of letters: [*intelligoque* and I understand *eandem diem* that the same time, *quam* which *spero* I hope *fore* will be *æternam* everlasting, *propagatam* has been extended *et* both *ad salutem* for the safety *urbis* of the city *et* and *ad memoriam* for the memory *mei consulatus* of my consulship;] *duosque cives* and that two citizens *extitisse* have appeared *uno tempore* at one time *in hac republica* in this republic, *quorum* of whom *alter* the one *terminaret* bounded *fines* the frontiers *vestri imperii* of your empire *non* not *regionibus* by the regions *terræ* of the earth, *sed* but

74

cœli of the sky, *alter* the other *servaret* kept safe *domicilium* the home *sedemque* and seat *ejusdem imperii* of the same empire.

XII. 27. *Sed* but *quoniam* since *fortuna* the fortune *atque conditio* and lot *earum rerum* of those things *quas* which *ego* I *gessi* have conducted, *non est* is not *eadem* the same *quæ* as *illorum* of those *qui* who *gesserunt* have carried on *externa bella* foreign wars, *quod* because *vivendum est mihi* I have to live *cum his* with these, *quos* whom *vici* I have conquered *ac subegi* and subdued, *isti* they *reliquerunt* have left *hostes* enemies *aut* either *interfectos* slain *aut* or *oppressos* crushed: *est* it is *vestrum* your duty, *Quirites* Romans, *si* if *sua facta* their own deeds *prosunt* are profitable *cæteris* to the others, *providere* to take care beforehand *mea* that my deeds *ne quando absint* may not at any time be an injury *mihi* to me. *Ego enim* for I *providi* have provided *sceleratæ* that the wicked *ac* and *nefariæ mentes* nefarious intentions *hominum audacissimorum* of most audacious men *ne possent* might not be able *nocere vobis* to hurt you: *vestrum est* it is yours *providere* to provide *ne noceant* that they may not do harm *mihi* to me. *Quanquam* although, *Quirites* Romans, *jam* now *nihil potest noceri* no harm can be done *mihi* to me *ab istis* by them: *est enim* for there is *magnum præsidium* a great protection *in bonis* in good men, *quod* which *comparatum est* has been procured *mihi* for me *in perpetuum* for ever; *magna dignitas* great dignity *in republica* in the republic, *quæ* which *semper defendet* will always defend *me* me *tacita* in silence: *est* there is *magna vis* great force *conscientiæ* in conscience, *quam* which *qui* those who *negligent* shall neglect, *ipsi indicabunt* will themselves show, *quum* when *volent* they shall wish *violare*
⁺ violate *me* me. 28. *Est etiam* there is also *in nobis* in me, *Quirites* Romans, *is animus* such a feeling, *ut* that *non modo cedamus* we not only yield *audaciæ* to

the audacity *nullius* of none, *sed etiam* but also *sem-*
per always *ultro* of our own accord *lacessamus* attack
omnes improbos all wicked men. *Quod si* but if
omnis impetus all the fury *domesticorum hostium* of
domestic enemies, *depulsus* warded off *a vobis* from
you, *converterit* shall have turned *se* itself *in me unum*
on me alone : *vobis* for you, *Quirites* Romans, *provi-*
dendum erit it will be needful to consider, *qua con-*
ditione in what condition *ve.'tis* you wish *eos* those
esse to be *posthac* hereafter, *qui* who *obtulerint* have
offered *se* themselves *invidiæ* to envy *maximisque*
periculis and to the greatest perils *pro salute vestra*
for your safety. *Mihi quidem* for me indeed *ipsi*
myself *quid* what *est* is there *quod* which *jam* now
possit can *acquiri* be acquired *ad fructum* to the enjoyment *vitæ* of life, *præsertim* especially *quum* when
videam I see *neque* neither *in honore vestro* in your
honour, *neque* nor *in gloria* in the glory *virtutis* of
virtue *quidquam* any thing *altius* higher *quo quidem*
whither indeed *libeat mihi* I may desire *ascendere*
to climb? 29. *Perficiam* I shall effect *illud* this
profecto no doubt, *Quirites* Romans, *ut tuear* to defend *atque ornem* and adorn *privatus* as a private
man *ea* those deeds *quæ* which *gessi* I performed *in*
consulatu in the consulship; *ut* that, *si* if *qua in-*
vidia any odium *suscepta est* has been incurred *in*
conservanda republica in preserving the republic,
lædat it may damage *invidos* those who envy me,
valeat [but] may serve *ad gloriam* for glory *mihi* to
me. *Denique* lastly *tractabo* I shall behave *me* myself *in republica* in the state *ita* so *ut semper memi-*
nerim as always to remember *quæ* what things *ges-*
serim I have done, *curemque* and take care *ut* that
videantur they may seem *gesta esse* to have been
done *virtute* by merit *non casu* not by chance. *Vos*
you, *Quirites* Romans, *quoniam* since *jam* now *est*
nox it is night, *veneramini* worship *illum Jovem* great
Jove, *custodem* guard *hujus urbis* of this city *ac*

76

vestrum and yours, *atque* and *discedite* depart *in vestra tecta* to your homes, *et* and *quanquam* although *periculum* the danger *jam depulsum est* is already warded off, *tamen* yet *defendite* defend *ea* those [homes] *custodiis* with guards *vigilisque* and watches *æque ac* the same as *priori nocte* last night. *Ne* lest *id* that *sit* may be *faciendum vobis* needful for you to do *diutius* any longer, *Quirites* Romans, *atque* and *ut* that *possitis* you may *esse* be *in perpetua pace* in perpetual quiet, *providebo* I will take care.

CATILINE IV.

Video I see, *patres conscripti* conscript fathers, *ora* that the looks *atque oculos* and eyes *omnium vestrum* of you all, *conversos esse* are turned *in me* on me. *Video* I see *vos* that you *sollicitos esse* are solicitous *non solum* not only *de vestro periculo* for your own danger *ac* and *reipublicæ* that of the republic, *verum etiam* but also, *si* if *id* that *depulsum sit* be warded off, *de meo* for mine [also]. *Vestra voluntas* your good will *erga me* towards me *jucunda est* is grateful *mihi* to me *in malis* amid evils *et grata* and pleasing *in dolore* in sorrow: *sed* but *per deos immortales* by the immortal gods *quæso* I beg of you *deponite eam* lay it aside *atque* and *obliti* forgetful *salutis meæ* of my safety *cogitate* think *de vobis* of yourselves *ac* and *de liberis vestris* of your children. *Si quidem* if indeed *hæc conditio* this condition *consulatus* of the consulship *data est* has been assigned *mihi* to me, *ut* that *perferrem* I should bear *omnes acerbitates* every bitterness, *omnes dolores* all hardships *cruciatusque* and sufferings; *feram* I will bear them *non solum* not only *fortiter* bravely *sed etiam* but also *libenter* cheerfully *dummodo* if only *meis laboribus* by my labours, *dignitas* dignity *salusque* and safety *pariatur* be procured *vobis* for you *Romanoque populo* and the

6

Roman people. *Ego sum* I am *ille consul* such a consul, *patres conscripti* conscript fathers, *cui* to whom *non forum* neither the forum *in quo* in which *omnis æquitas* all justice *continetur* is contained, *non campus* nor the Campus Martius *consecratus* consecrated *consularibus auspiciis* by consular auspices; *non curia* nor the senate house, *summum auxilium* the chief refuge *omnium gentium* of all nations; *non domus* nor my own home, *commune perfugium* the common asylum [of all men]; *non lectus* nor the bed *datus* destined *ad quietem* to repose; *deinque* lastly *non* not [even] *hæc sedes* this seat *honoris* of honour, *fuit* has been *unquam* ever *vacua* safe *periculo* from the danger *mortis* of death, *atque insidiis* and treachery. *Ego* I *tacui* have been silent about *multa* many things; *pertuli* I have endured *multa* many things; *concessi* I have yielded *multa* many things; *sanavi* I have quieted *multa* many things, *in vestro timore* in the midst of your alarm *meo quodam dolore* with a sort of grief on my part. *Nunc* now *si* if *dii immortales* the immortal gods *voluerunt* have willed *hanc* that this *esse* should be *exitum* the issue *consulatus mei* of my consulship, *ut* that *eriperem* I should save *vos* you, *patres conscripti* conscript fathers, *populumque Romanum* and the Roman people *ex cæde miserrimâ* from a most wretched slaughter; *conjuges* your wives, *liberosque vestros* and your children, *virginesque vestales* and the vestal virgins *ex acerbissima vexatione* from the most cruel outrages; *templa* the temples *atque delubra* and the shrines [of the gods] *hanc pulcherrimam patriam* [and] this most beautiful country *omnium nostrum* of all of us, *ex fædissima flamma* from horrible flames; *totam Italiam* the whole of Italy *ex bello* from war *et vastitate* and desolation; *quæcunque fortuna* whatever fortune *proponetur* shall be proposed *mihi uni* for me alone *subeatur* let it be undergone. *Etenim* for *si* if *Publius Lentulus* Publius Lentulus *inductus* induced

78

a vatibus by the prophets *putavit* thought *suum nomen* that his name *fore* would be *fatale* fated *ad perniciem* to the destruction *reipublicæ* of the republic, *cur* why *ego non læter* should I not rejoice *meum consulatum* that my consulship *exstitisse* has appeared *prope* almost *fatale* destined *ad salutem* for the safety *reipublicæ* of the commonwealth.

II. *Quare* wherefore, *conscripti patres* conscript fathers, *consulite* consult *vobis* for yourselves, *prospicite* provide for *patriæ* your country, *conservate* secure *vos* yourselves, *conjuges* your wives, *liberos* your children, *fortunasque vestras* and your fortunes ; *defendite* guard *nomen* the name *salutemque* and the safety *Romani populi* of the Roman people ; *desinite* cease *parcere* to show consideration *mihi* for me *ac* and *cogitare* to think *de me* about me. *Nam* for *debeo sperare* I must hope *omnes deos* that all the gods, *qui* who *president* preside over *huic urbi* this city, *relaturos esse* will repay *gratiam* gratitude *mihi* to me *pro eo* for such *ac* as *mereor* I deserve : *deinde* then *si quid* if anything *obtigerit* shall befall me, *moriar* I shall die *æquo* with calm *paratoque animo* and ready mind. *Neque enim* for neither *potest* can *turpis mors* a disgraceful death *accidere* happen *forti viro* to a brave man, *neque* nor *immatura* an untimely one *consulari* to one who has been consul, *neque* nor *misera* a wretched one *sapienti* to a wise man. *Nec tamen* yet neither *ego sum* am I *ille ferreus* so iron-hearted *qui non movear* as not to be moved *mœrore* by the grief *carissimi* of my most dear *atque* and *amantissimi fratris* loving brother, *præsentis* who is here present, *lacrymisque* and by the tears *omnium horum* of all these, *a quibus* by whom *videtis* you see *me* me *circumsessum* surrounded ; *neque* nor *uxor* does my wife *exanimata* half dead with terror, *non sæpe* not often *revocat* recall *meam mentem* my mind *domum* to home, *filia* and my daughter *abjecta* cast down *metu* by fear, *et* and

79

parvulus filius my infant son, *quem* whom *respublica* the republic *videtur* seems *mihi* to me *amplecti* to hold in its arms *tamquam* as *obsidem* a pledge *consulatus mei* of my consulship: *neque* nor *ille gener* does that son-in-law *qui* who *exspectans* waiting for *exitum* the result *hujus diei* of this day *adstat* is present *in meo conspectu* in my sight. *Moveor* I am moved *his omnibus rebus* by all these things, *sed* but *in eam partem* in this direction *ut* that *omnes* all sint may be *salvi* safe *vobiscum* along with you, *etiamsi* even if *aliqua vis* some act of violence *oppresserit me* may have crushed me, *potius quam* rather than *et illi* that both they *et nos* and we *una cum republica* together with the republic *pereamus* should perish. *Quare* wherefore, *conscripti patres* conscript fathers, *incumbite* bend yourselves *ad salutem* to the safety *reipublicæ* of the republic: *circumspicite* look round on *omnes procellas* all the storms *quæ* which *impendent* threaten us *nisi* unless *providetis* you provide against them. *Non Tiberius Gracchus* neither Tiberius Gracchus, *qui* who *voluit* wished *fieri* to become *iterum* a second time *tribunus* tribune *plebis* of the commons: *non Caius Gracchus* nor Caius Gracchus *qui* who *conatus est* endeavoured *concitare* to excite *agrarios* the Agrarian party, *non Lucius Saturninus* nor Lucius Saturninus *qui* who *occidit* slew *Caium Memmium* Caius Memmius *adducitur* is now being brought *in discrimen aliquod* into any danger *atque* and *ad judicium* to the sentence *vestræ severitatis* of your severity; *ii* they *tenentur* are held in custody *qui* who *restiterunt* remained *Romæ* at Rome *ad urbis incendium* to burn the city, *ad vestram omnium cædem* to massacre all of you, *ad Catilinam accipiendum* and to receive Catiline: *litteræ* their letters, *signa* their seals, *manus* their hands, *denique* in short *confessio* the confession *uniuscujusque* of each *tenentur* are in our possession; *Allobroges* the Allobroges *sollicitantur* are tampered with: *servitia* the slaves *excitantur* are excited to insurrection; *Catilina* Catiline *arcessitur* is sent for: *id est* this is *consilium* the design *initum* entered upon *ut* that *omnibus interfectis* all being slain *nemo* nobody *relinquatur* should be left *ad deplorandum* to lament *nomen* the name *reipublicæ* of the commonwealth *atque* and *lamentandam calamitatem* to lament the overthrow *tanti imperii* of so great an empire.

III. 5. *Hæc omnia* all these things *indices* the witnesses *detulerunt* have reported; *rei* the accused *confessi sunt* have confessed, *vos* you *jam* already *iudicastis* have decided *multis judiciis* by several judgments: *primum* first *quod* because *egistis gratias* you have returned thanks *mihi* to me *singularibus verbis* in an unusual form of words; *et decrevistis* and you have declared *mea virtute* that by my public spirit *atque vigilentia* and vigilance *conjurationem* the conspiracy *perditorum hominum* of these desperate men *patefactum esse* has been laid open: *deinde* next *quod* because *coëgistis* you have compelled *Publium Lentulum* Publius Lentulus *ut se abdicaret* to abdicate *prætura* his prætorship *tum* then *quod* because *censuistis* you have decreed *eum* him *et ceteros* and the rest *de quibus* about whom *judicastis* you have pronounced judgment *dandos* to be given *in custodiam* into custody: *maximeque* and chiefly *quod* because *decrevistis* you have decreed *supplicationem* a thanksgiving *meo nomine* in my name, *qui honos* which honour *habitus est* was shown *nemini* to no one *togaio* who has worn the toga *ante me* before me: *postremo* lastly *hesterno die* yesterday *dedistis* you gave *amplissima præmia* most ample rewards *legatis* to the ambassadors *Allobrogum* of the Allobrogians *Titoque Vulturcio* and Titus Vulturcius: *quæ omnia* all which things *sunt* are *ejusmodi* of such a nature *ut* that *ii* those *qui* who *dati sunt* are given *nominatim* nominally *in custodiam* into custody *videantur* seem *damnati esse* to have been condemned *a vobis* by you *sine ulla dubitatione* without any hesitation. *Sed ego* but I *institui* have resolved *patres conscripti* conscript fathers *referre* to refer *ad vos* to you *tamquam* as if *integrum* afresh *et* both *de facto* concerning the affair itself *quid* what *judicetis* you judge *et* and *de pœna* concerning the punishment *quid* what *censeatis* you determine. *Prædicam* I will first speak of *illa* those [duties] *quæ* which *sunt* are [the duties] *consulis* of a consul. *Ego* I *jampridem videbam* had long been seeing *magnum furorem* a great madness *versari* to be prevalent *in republica* in the republic *et* and *quædam mala* certain evils *nova* unknown *misceri* to be aroused *et concitari* and stirred up: *sed* but *nunquam putavi* I never thought *conjurationem* that a conspiracy *tantam* so great *tam exitiosam* so dreadful *haberi* was entertained *a civibus* by the citizens. *Nunc* now *quidquid est* whatever it is *quocumque* which ever way *vestræ mentes* your minds *atque* and *sententiæ* opinions *inclinant* incline, *statuendum est vobis* you must determine *ante noctem* before night. *Videtis* you see *quantum facinus* how great a crime *delatum sit* has been reported *ad vos* to you. *Si* if *putatis* you think *paucos* that [only] a few *affines esse* are attached *huic* to this, *erratis* you err *vehementer* greatly. *Hoc malum* this mischief *disseminatum est* is spread *latius* wider *opinione* than is thought: *non solum* not only *manavit* has it spread *per Italiam* throughout Italy *sed etiam* but also *transcendit* crossed *Alpes* the Alps *et* and *serpens* creeping *obscure* secretly *occupavit* seized *multas provincias* many provinces: *id* it *potest* can *opprimi* be suppressed *nullo pacto* in no way *sustentando* by tolerating *ac prolatando* and delaying. *Quacunque ratione* in whatever manner *placet* it pleases *vobis* you *vindicandum est* you must take vengeance *celeriter* quickly.

IV. *Video* I see ~~~ that there are *adhuc* as yet

auas sententias two opinions: *unam* the one *Decimi Silani* of Decimus Silänus *qui* who *censet* thinks, *eos* that these *qui* who *conati sunt* have endeavoured *delere* to destroy *hæc* this state of things *multandos esse* ought to be punished *morte* by death: *alteram* the other *Caii Cæsaris* of Julius Cæsar, *qui* who *removet* puts aside *pœnam* the punishment *mortis* of death, *amplectitur* but embraces *omnes acerbitates* all the severities *ceterorum suppliciorum* of the other punishments. *Uterque* each of the two *et* both *pro sua dignitate* in proportion to his dignity, *et pro magnitudine* and to the greatness *rerum* of things *versatur* dwells *in summa severitate* on the greatest severity. *Alter* the one *putat* thinks *non oportere* that it is not becoming *eos* that those *qui* who *conati sunt* have endeavoured *privare* to deprive *nos omnes* all of us *qui* who [have endeavoured to deprive] *populum Romanum* the Roman people *vita* of life, *qui* who [have endeavoured] *delere* to obliterate *imperium* the empire, *qui* who [have endeavoured] *exstinguere* to extinguish *nomen* the name *Romani populi* of the Roman people *frui* should enjoy *vita et* and *hoc spiritu* this air *communi* common to men *punctum temporis* for a moment of time; *eaque recordatur* and he remembers *hoc genus* that this sort *pœnæ* of punishment *sæpe usurpatum esse* has often been employed *in hac republica* in this republic *in improbos cives* against seditious citizens. *Alter* the other *intelligit* understands *mortem* that death *non constitutam esse* was not designed *a diis immortalibus* by the immortal gods *causa* for the sake *supplicii* of punishment *sed* but *esse* is *aut* either *necessitatem* a necessity *naturæ* of nature *aut* or *quietem* a cessation *laborum* of toils *ac* and *miseriarum* miseries. *Itaque* therefore *sapientes* the wise *nunquam* never *oppetiverunt* have met *eam* it *inviti* unwillingly, *fortes* the brave *sæpe* often *libenter* voluntarily. *Vincula vero* imprisonment however *ea sempiterna* and that too for life *inventa sunt* was invented *certe* certainly *ad singularem pœnam* for the express punishment *nefarii sceleris* of abandoned guilt. *Jubet* he urges upon us *dispertiri* that they should be dispersed *municipiis* throughout the municipal towns. *Ista res* that proposition of yours *videtur* seems *habere* to have *iniquitatem* injustice *si* if *velis* you wish *imperare* to demand it; *difficultatem* difficulty *si* if *rogare* to ask it: *tamen* yet *decernatur* let it be decreed *si* if *placet* it pleases you. *Ego enim* for I *suscipiam* will undertake *et* and, *ut* as *spero* I hope, *reperiam* will find [men] *qui* who *non putent* do not think it *suæ dignitatis* consistent with their dignity *recusare* to refuse *id* that *quod* which *statueritis* you shall have determined *causâ* for the cause *salutis* of the safety *omnium* of all. *Adjungit* he adds *gravem pœnam* a heavy punishment *municipibus* on the municipal towns, *si* if *quis* anyone *eorum* of them *ruperit* should have burst *vincula* their bond: *circumdat* he throws round them *horribiles custodias* frightful imprisonments *et* and *sancit* sanctions *digna* whatever is worthy *scelere* of the guilt *hominum perditorum* of abandoned wretches, *ne quis* so that no one *possit* may be able *aut* either *per senatum* through the senate *aut* or *per populum* through the people *levare* to mitigate *pœnam* the punishment *eorum* of those *quos* whom *condemnat* he is condemning. *Eripit etiam* he also takes away *spem* the hope *quæ* which *sola* alone *solet* is wont *consolari* to console *hominem* a man *in miseriis* in misery. *Præterea* moreover *jubet* he bids *bona* their estates *publicari* to be confiscated: *relinquit* he leaves *vitam* life *solam* alone *nefariis hominibus* to these impious men: *quam* which *si* if *eripuisset* he had taken away *ademisset* he would have taken from [them] *uno dolore* by one pang *multos dolores* many pangs *animi* of mind *atque* and *corporis* of body *et omnes pœnas* and all the punishments *scelerum* of their crimes. *Itaque* therefore *ut*

84

that *esset* there might be *aliqua formido* some fear *posita* established *improbis* for the wicked *in vita* in life, *illi antiqui* these men of old times *voluerunt* willed *quædam supplicia* that certain punishments *ejusmodi* of that kind *constituta esse* were appointed *impiis* for the wicked *apud inferos* in the lower world, *quod* because *videlicet* no doubt *intelligebant* they perceived *his remotis* [that] if these were removed *ipsam mortem* death itself *non esse pertimescendam* was not to be feared.

V. *Nunc* now, *patres conscripti* conscript fathers, *ego video* I see *quid* how *mea intersit* my interests are concerned. *Si* if *eritis secuti* you will follow *sententiam* the opinion *Caii Cæsaris* of Caius Cæsar, *quoniam* since *is* he *secutus est* has pursued *hanc viam* such a career *in republica* in public affairs, *quæ* which *habetur* is held to be *popularis* popular, *fortasse* perhaps *impetus populares* popular assaults, *hoc auctore* he being the author *et* and *cognitore* supporter *hujusce sententiæ* of this opinion, *erunt* will be *minus* less *pertimescendi* alarming *mihi* to me? *Sin* but if *illam alteram* the other one *nescio* I know not *an* whether *amplius negotii* additional trouble *contrahatur* may [not] be gathered *mihi* for me. *Sed tamen* but yet *utilitas* let the interest *reipublicæ* of the republic *vincat* overcome *rationes* the considerations *meorum periculorum* of my own dangers, *habemus enim* for we have *a Caio Cæsare* from Caius Cæsar, *sicut* as *ipsius dignitas* his own high rank *et* and *amplitudo* the merits *majorum* of his ancestors *postulabat* required, *sententiam* an opinion *tamquam* as it were *obsidem* a pledge *perpetuæ voluntatis* of perpetual affection *in rempublicam* to the state : *intellectum est* it has been seen *quid intersit* what difference there is *inter levitatem* between the insincerity *concionatorum* of public declaimers *et* and *animum* a spirit *vere* truly *popularem* attached to the people *consulentem* consulting *saluti* for the safety *populi* of the nation.

Video I see *de istis* that out of those *qui* who *volunt* wish *se* themselves *haberi* to be thought *populares* popular, *non neminem* that a certain person *abesse* is absent, *videlicet* forsooth *ne ferat* that he may not give *sententiam* his vote *de capite* on the life *civium Romanorum* of Roman citizens. *Is* he *nudiustertius* three days ago *et* both *dedit* gave *in custodiam* into custody *cives Romanos* Roman citizens *et decrevit mihi* and decreed for me *supplicationem* a thanksgiving *et hesterno die* and yesterday *affecit* honoured *maximis præmiis* with the most ample rewards *indices* the informers. *Jam* now *hoc* this *dubium est* is doubtful *nemini* to no one *quid* what *judicarit* he judged *de tota re* on the whole matter *et* and *causa* cause *qui* who *decrevit* decreed *custodiam* imprisonment *reo* to the accused, *gratulationem* thanks *quæsitori* to the discoverer [of the conspiracy], *præmium* and a reward *indici* to the informer. *At vero* but indeed *Caius Cæsar* Caius Cæsar *intelligit* understands *legem Semproniam* that the Sempronian law *constitutam esse* was enacted *de civibus Romanis* about the Roman citizens; *eum autem* but that he *qui* who *sit* is *hostis* an enemy *reipublicæ* of the state *posse* can *nullo modo* in no respect *esse* be considered *civem* as a citizen: *denique* and finally *ipsum latorem* that the very proposer himself *legis Semproniæ* of the Sempronian law *defendisse* rendered *pœnas* atonement *reipublicæ* to the state *jussu* by the order *populi* of the people. *Idem* the same individual *non putat* does not think *Lentulum* that Lentulus *ipsum* himself, *largitorem* a squanderer *et prodigum* and prodigal *quum* when *cogitarit* he concerted *tam acerbe* so bitterly *tamque crudeliter* and so cruelly *de pernicie* for the destruction *populi Romani* of the Roman people *et* and *exitio* the destruction *hujus urbis* of this city, *posse* can *appellari* be called *popularem* a popular man. *Itaque* therefore *homo* a man *mitissimus* most mild *atque lenissi-*

86

mus and merciful *non dubitat* makes no scruple *mandare* to condemn *Publium Lentulum* Publius Lentulus *æternis tenebris* to perpetual darkness *vinculisque* and imprisonment, *et sancit* and provides *ne quis* that no one *in posterum* for the future *possit* may have it in his power *jactare* to boast *se* himself *levando* by lightening *supplicio* the punishment *hujus* of this man *et* and *esse* to be *popularis* popular *in pernicie* amid the destruction *populi Romani* of the Roman people. *Etiam adjungit* he also adds *publicationem* the confiscation *bonorum* of their goods *ut* that *etiam egestas* want also *ac* and *mendicitas* beggary *consequatur* may attend *omnes cruciatus* every torment *animi* of mind *et corporis* and body.

VI. *Quamobrem* wherefore *sive* whether *statueritis* you shall have decreed *hoc* this, *dederitis mihi* you will have given me *comitem* a companion *ad concionem* for the public assembly *carum* dear *atque jucundum* and acceptable *populo* to the people; *sive* or if *malueritis* you prefer *sequi* to follow *sententiam* the opinion *Silani* of Silanus *facile defendetis* you will easily defend *me* me *atque vos* and you *a vituperatione* from the imputation *crudelitatis* of cruelty, *atque* and *obtinebo* I shall obtain *eam* that it *fuisse* has been *multo leniorem* much more merciful. *Quanquam* although, *patres conscripti* conscript fathers, *quæ crudelitas* what cruelty *potest esse* can there be *in punienda immanitate* in punishing the atrocity *tanti sceleris* of so great a crime? *Ego enim* for I *judico* judge *de meo sensu* from my own feelings. *Nam* for *ita* so *liceat* may it be allowed *mihi* to me *perfrui* to enjoy *republica* the republic *salva* in safety *vobiscum* together with you, *ut* as *ego* I, *quod sum* in that I am *vehementior* somewhat vehement *in hac causa* in this cause, *moveor* am influenced *non* not *atrocitate* by atrocity *animi* of mind, *sed* but *singulari quadam humanitate* by a singular humanity *et misericordia* and by mercy: (*quis enim* for

87

who *est* is *mitior* more gentle *me* than I ?) *Videor enim* for I seem *mihi* to myself *videre* to see *hanc urbem* this city, *lucem* the light *orbis* of the globe *terrarum* of the earth *atque* and *arcem* the citadel *omnium gentium* of all nations, *concidentem* falling *subito* suddenly *uno incendio* by one conflagration; *cerno* I perceive *animo* in my mind *acervos* heaps *civium* of my countrymen *miseros* wretched *atque insepultos* and unburied *in patria sepulta* in my buried country : *aspectus* the look *et furor* and the fury *Cethegi* of Cethegus *bacchantis* revelling *in vestra cæde* in your blood *versatur* flits *ante oculos mihi* before my eyes. 12. *Quum vero* but when *proposui mihi* I have pictured to myself *Lentulum* Lentulus *regnantem* reigning, *sicut* as *ipse* himself *confessus est* confessed *se* that he *sperasse* had hopes *ex fatis* from the [Sibylline] prophecies, *hunc Gabinium* that this Gabinius *purpuratum esse* was arrayed in purple; *Catilinam* that Catiline *venisse* had come *cum exercitu* with an army, *tum* then *perhorresco* I shudder at *lamentionem* the lamentation *matrumfamilias* of the mothers of families, *tum* then *fugam* the flight *virginum* of virgins *atque* and *puerorum* of boys, *ac* and *vexationem* the harassing *virginum Vestalium* of the Vestal virgins : *et* and *quia* because *hæc* these things *videntur* seem *mihi* to me *vehementer misera* exceedingly wretched *atque miseranda* and pitiable, *idcirco* therefore *præbeo* I show *me* myself *severum* severe *vehementemque* and stern *in eos* towards those *qui* who *voluerunt* have wished *perficere* to effect *ea* those doings. *Etenim quæro* and I wish to know, *si* if *quis paterfamilias* any father of a family, *liberis suis interfectis* when his children have been slain *a servo* by his slave, *uxore* his wife *occisa* put to death, *domo incensa* his house burnt, *non sumpserit supplicium* shall not exact punishment *quam acerbissimum* the most severe possible *de servis* of his slaves, *utrum* whether *is* he *videatur* must be thought *clemens* mild *ac misericors* and merciful *an* or *inhu-manissimus* most inhuman *et* and *crudelissimus* most cruel? *Mihi vero* to me indeed *importunus* [he will be thought] untoward *ac ferreus* and iron[hearted] *qui* who *non lenierit* shall not have assuaged *suum dolorem* his own pain *cruciatumque* and torment *dolore* by the pain *ac cruciatu* and torment *nocentis* of the guilty man. *Sic* thus *nos* we—*in his hominibus* in the case of these men, *qui* who *voluerunt* have wished *trucidare* to slay *nos* us, *qui conjuges* our wives, *qui liberos nostros* our children, *qui* who *conati sunt* have endeavoured *delere* to destroy *singulas domos* the several houses *uniuscujusque* of each one of us *et* and *hoc universum domicilium* this general home *reipublicæ* of the republic, *qui* who *id egerunt* had this object *ut* that *collocarent* they might place *gentem* the nation *Allobrogum* of the Allobroges *in vestigiis* on the traces *hujus urbis* of this city *atque* and *in cinere* on the ashes *deflagrati imperii* of the empire destroyed by fire, *habebimur* shall be reckoned *misericordes* merciful *si* if *fuerimus* we shall be *vehementissimi* most severe, *sin* but if *voluerimus* we shall wish *esse* to be *remissiores* more lenient, *fama* the reputation *summæ crudelitatis* of the utmost cruelty *subeunda est* must be encountered *nobis* by us *in pernicie* in the destruction *patriæ* of our country *civiumque* and our citizens.

13. *Nisi vero* unless indeed *Lucius Cæsar* Lucius Cæsar, *vir fortissimus* a most brave man *et* and *amantissimus* a most loyal subject *reipublicæ* of the republic, *visus est* seemed *cuipiam* to any one *crudelior* somewhat cruel *nudiustertius* the day before yesterday, *quum* when *dixit* he said *virum* that the husband *sororis suæ* of his sister, *feminæ lectissimæ* a most choice woman, *præsentem* being present *atque audientem* and hearing what he said, *privandum esse* ought to be deprived *vita* of life, *quum* when *dixit* he said *avum* that his grandfather *interfectum* was

put to death *jussu* by command *consulis* of the consul, *filiumque ejus* and that his son *impuberem* still
beardless, *missum* who had been sent *legatum* legate
a patre by his father, *necatum esse* had been slain
in carcere in prison. *Quorum* of whom *quod factum*
what crime [was there] *simile* like this one? *quod
consilium* what design *delendæ reipublicæ* of destroy-
ing the republic *initum* entered upon [by them]? *Voluntas* the desire *largitionis* of bribery *et* and *quædam
contentio* a contest *partium* of parties *tum* at that
time *versata est* resided *in republica* in the republic.
Atque and *illo tempore* at that time *avus* the grandfather *hujus Lentuli* of this Lentulus, *vir clarissimus*
a man of much distinction, *persecutus est* pursued
armatus in arms *Gracchum* Gracchus: *ille* he [the
grandfather] *etiam* even *tum* then *accepit* received
grave vulnus a severe wound *ne quid minueretur* that
no diminution might be made *de summa dignitate* from
the supreme dignity *reipublicæ* of the republic, *hic*
this man [Lentulus] *ad evertenda fundamenta* in
order to undermine the foundations *reipublicæ* of the
republic *arcessit* sends for *Gallos* the Gauls, *concitat*
stirs up *servitia* the slaves, *vocat* invites *Catilinam*
Catiline, *attribuit* gives over *nos* us *trucidandos* to be
slain *Cethego* to Cethegus, *cæteros cives* the rest of
the citizens *interficiendos* to be put to death *Gabinio*
to Gabinius, *urbem* the city *inflammandam* to be fired
Cassio to Cassius, *totam Italiam* the whole of Italy
vastandam to be ravaged *diripiendamque* and to be
plundered *Catilinæ* to Catiline. *Veremini* you fear,
censeo I think, *ne* lest *in hoc scelere* in the case of
this crime *tam immani* so huge *ac nefando* and abominable *videamini* you may seem *statuisse* to have
decreed *aliquid* something *nimis severe* too severely;
cuum whereas *sit* it is *multo magis verendum* much
more to be feared *ne* lest *remissione* by the remission
pœnæ of punishment *videamur* we may seem *fuisse*
to have been *crudeles* cruel *in patriam* towards our

country *quam* than *ne* lest [we may seem to have been] *nimis vehementes* too violent *severitate* by the severity *animadversionis* of punishment *in acerbissimos hostes* against the bitterest enemies.

VII. 14. *Sed* but *non possum* I am not able, *patre sconscripti* conscript fathers, *dissimulare* to dissemble *ea* those things *quæ* which *exaudio* I hear. *Jaciuntur enim* for there are cast about *voces* words *quæ* which *perveniunt* arrive *ad aures meas* to my ears, *eorum* of those *qui* who *videntur* seem *vereri* to be afraid, *ut habeam* [wishing] that I may have *satis præsidii* guard strong enough *ad ea transigunda* to execute those things *quæ* which *vos* you *statueritis* shall have decreed *hodierno die* this day. *Omnia* all things, *patres conscripti* conscript fathers, *sunt* are *et provisa* both provided *et parata* and prepared *et constituta* and appointed, *quum* not only *mea summa cura* by my chief care *atque diligentia* and diligence, *tum* but also *etiam multo majore voluntate* by the even greater will *populi Romani* of the Roman people *ad retinendum* to retain *summum imperium* the supreme authority *et* and *ad conservandas* to preserve *communes fortunas* our common fortunes. *Omnes homines* all men *omnium ordinum* of all classes, *denique* and in short *omnium ætatum* of all ages, *adsunt* are present: *forum* the forum *plenum est* is full; *templa* the temples *circa forum* round the forum *plena* are full; *omnes aditus* all the approaches *hujus loci* of this place *ac templi* and temple *pleni* are full. *Hæc enim* for this *est* is *sola causa* the only cause *inventa* that has been found *post urbem conditam* since the building of the city, *in qua* in which *omnes* all men *sentirent* had an opinion *unum* one *atque idem* and the same, *præter eos* except those *qui* who, *quum* when *viderent* they saw *sibi esse pereundum* that they must perish, *voluerunt* were willing *perire* to perish *cum omnibus* in company with all *potius rather quam soli* than alone. 15. *Ego* I *excipio* ex-

cept *hosce homines* these men *et secerno* and separate
them *libenter* willingly : *neque enim* for neither *puto*
do I think *habendos* that they are to be held *in numero* among the number *improborum·civium* of bad
citizens, *sed* but *in* among [that] *acerbissimorum
hostium* of most bitter enemies. *Cæteri vero* but the
rest, *dii immortales* immortal gods ! *qua frequentia*
in what a crowd, *quo studio* with what zeal, *qua
virtute* with what virtue *consentiunt* do they agree
together *ad communem dignitatem* for the common
dignity *salutemque* and safety ! *Quid* why *ego hic
commemorem* should I here speak of *equites Romanos*
the Roman knights ? *qui* who *concedunt* concede
vobis to you *summam* the chief place *ordinis* of
rank *consiliique* and of wisdom *ita* in such wise *ut*
that *certent* they may contend *vobiscum* with you
de amore for love *reipublicæ* of the republic : *quos*
whom *revocatos* having been recalled *ex dissensione*
from the dissension *multorum annorum* of many
years *ad societatem* to the society *concordiamque* and
concord *hujus ordinis* of this order, *hodiernus dies*
this day *atque* and *hæc causa* this cause *conjungit*
unites *vobiscum* with you : *quam conjunctionem*
which union *si* if *tenuerimus* we shall maintain *con-
firmatam* confirmed *in meo consulatu* in my consulship *perpetuam* for ever *in republica* in the republic,
confirmo vobis I assure you *nullum malum* that no
evil *posthac* hereafter *civile* civil *ac domesticum* and
domestic *venturum* will come *ad ullam partem* on
any part *reipublicæ* of the republic.

Video I see *tribunos ærarios* that the tribunes of
the treasury, *fortissimos viros* men of the staunchest
character, *convenisse* have come together *pari studio*
with like zeal *defendendæ reipublicæ* for defending
the republic ; *item* also *universos scribas* all the
scribes, *quos* whom *quum* when *hæc dies* this day
frequentasset had brought in great numbers *ad æra-*
    the treasury, *video* I see *conversos esse t*

⌐ attention has been turned *ab expectatione* from the expectation *sortis* of their stock *ad communem salutem* to the common safety. 16. *Omnis multi-tudo* the whole multitude *ingenuorum* of free men *etiam* even *tenuissimorum* of the poorest *adest* is present. *Quis enim* for who *est* is there *cui* to whom *hæc templa* these temples, *aspectus* the look *urbis* of the city, *possessio* the possession *libertatis* of liberty, *denique* and lastly *hæc lux* this light *ipsa* itself *et* and *hoc commune solum* this common soil *sit* is *quum* not only *carum* dear, *tum vero* but also *dulce* sweet *atque jucundum* and pleasant.

VIII. *Est* it is *pretium operæ* worth while, *patres conscripti* conscript fathers, *cognoscere* to learn *studia* the inclinations *libertinorum hominum* of our freed men; *qui* who, *virtute sua* by their merit *consequuti* having obtained *fortunam* the fortune *civitatis* of citizenship, *judicant* judge *hanc* this *esse* to be *vere* truly *patriam suam* their country; *quam quidem* which indeed *quidam* some *nati* born *hinc* from this place *et nati* and born *summo loco* in a high position *judicaverunt* have judged *esse* to be *non* not *patriam suam* their country, *sed* but *urbem* a city *hostium* of enemies. *Sed* but *quid* why *ego commemorem* should I speak of *homines* men *hujusce ordinis* of this order, *quos* whom *privatæ fortunæ* their private fortunes, *quos* whom *communis respublica* the common republic, *quos* whom *denique* lastly *libertas ea* that liberty, *quæ* which *est* is *dulcissima* most sweet, *excitavit* has roused *ad defendendam salutem* to defend the safety *patriæ* of their country? *Est* there is *nemo* no one *servus* a slave, *qui sit* provided he is *modo* only *tolerabili conditione* in a tolerable lot *servitutis* of slavery, *qui* who *non perhorrescat* does not shudder at *audaciam* the audacity *civium* of these citizens, *qui* who *non capiat* does not desire *hæc* that these things *stare* may stand; *qui* who *non conferat* does not contribute *tantum* as much *quantum* as *audet* he dares *et* and *quantum* as much as *potest* he can *ad communem salutem* to the common safety *civitatis* of the state. 17. *Quare* wherefore *si* if *hoc* this, *quod* which *auditum est* has been heard, *forte* by chance *commovet* moves *quem* any one *vestrum* of you, *lenonem quendam* that a certain pander *Lentuli* of Lentulus's *concursare* runs about *circum tabernas* from shop to shop, *sperare* and hopes *animos* that the minds *egentium* of the needy *atque imperitorum* and ignorant *posse* may *sollicitari* be stirred *pretio* by a bribe: *id quidem* that indeed *cœptum est* has been begun *atque tentatum* and tried: *sed* but *nulli* none *inventi sunt* have been found *aut* either *tam miseri* so wretched *fortuna* in fortune *aut* or *perditi* abandoned *voluntate* in their will, *qui* who *non velint* do not wish *ipsum illum locum* that very place *sellæ* of their seat *atque operis* and work *et* and *quæstus quotidiani* of daily gain, *qui* who *non* do not [wish] *cubile suum* their chamber *ac lectulum* and bed, *qui* who *denique* in short *non* do not [wish] *hunc cursum otiosum* this quiet course *vitæ suæ* of their life *esse* to be *salvum* safe. *Multo vero* but by far *maxima pars* the greatest part *eorum* of those *qui* who *sunt* are *in tabernis* in the shops, *immo vero* nay indeed (*id enim* for that *potius* rather *est dicendum* is to be said) *genus hoc universum* all this class *amantissimum est* is most fond *otii* of tranquillity. *Etenim* for also *omne eorum instrumentum* their whole apparatus *omnis opera* all their employment *ac quæstus* and gain *sustinetur* is sustained *frequentia* by the multitude *civium* of the citizens, *alitur* is nourished *otio* by tranquillity: *quorum quæstus* whose gain *si* if *solet* it is accustomed *minui* to be lessened *occlusis tabernis* by the shops being shut, *quid* what *futurum est* is likely to happen *tandem* at length *incensis* if they are burnt?

18. *Quæ* which things *quum ita sint* being so,

patres conscripti conscript fathers, *præsidia* the de-fences *populi Romani* of the Roman people *non ae-sunt* are not wanting *vobis* to you; *vos* do you *pro-videte* take precautions *ne videamini* that you may not seem *deesse* to be wanting *populo Romano* to the Roman people. IX. *Habetis* you have *consulem* a consul *reservatum* saved *ex plurimis periculis* from very many dangers *et insidiis* and snares *atque* and *ex media morte* from the midst of death *non* not *ad vitam suam* for his own life, *sed* but *ad salutem ves-tram* for your safety : *omnes ordines* all ranks *con-sentiunt* agree *mente* in mind, *voluntate* in will, *studio* in zeal, *virtute* in good service, *voce* with acclama-tion *ad conservandam rempublicam* to preserve the state; *patria communis* our common country *obsessa* blockaded *facibus* with the torches *et telis* and weapons *impiæ conjurationis* of an unholy con-spiracy, *supplex* suppliant *tendit* stretches forth *manus* her hands *vobis* to you; *commendat* she in-trusts *se* herself *vobis* to you, *vitam* the life *omnium civium* of all her citizens *vobis* to you, *vobis* to you *arcem* the citadel *et* and *capitolium* the capitol, *vobis* to you *aras* the altars *penatium* of our penates, *vobis* to you *illum perpetuum* that perpetual *ac* and *sempiternum ignem* everlasting fire *Vestæ* of Vesta, *vobis* to you *omnia templa* all the temples *atque de-lubra* and shrines *deorum* of the gods, *vobis* to you *muros* the walls *atque tecta* and houses *urbis* of the city. *Præterea* moreover *judicandum est vobis* you have to determine *hodierno die* this day *de vestra vita* about your existence *de anima* about the life *vestrarum conjugum* of your wives *ac liberorum* and children *de fortunis* about the fortunes *omnium* of all, *de sedibus vestris* about your homes, *de focis* about your hearths. 19. *Habetis* you have *ducem* a leader *memorem* mindful *vestri* of you, *oblitum* for-getful *sui* of himself; *quæ facultas* which facility *non semper datur* is not always afforded; *habetis*

95

you have *omnes ordines* all ranks, *omnes homines* all men, *universum populum Romanum* all the Roman people, (*id quod* a thing which *primum videmus* we first see *hodierno die* this day *in civili causa* in any civil trial) *sentientem* thinking *unum* one *atque idem* and the same. *Cogitate* think, *quantis laboribus* on what great labours *fundatum* founded *imperium* our empire, *quanta virtute* on what valour *stabilitam* established *libertatem* our liberty, *quanta benignitate* on what great benevolence *deorum* of the gods *auctas* increased *exaggeratasque* and multiplied *fortunas* our fortunes *una nox* one night *pæne delerit* has almost destroyed. *Providendum est* you must provide *hodierno die* this day, *id* that this *ne possit* may not *posthac* hereafter *non modo* not only *confici* be done, *sed* but *ne cogitari quidem* not even be thought of *a civibus* by our citizens. *Atque* and *loquutus sum* I have spoken *hæc* these words *non* not, *ut* that *excitarem* I might stir up *vos* you, *qui* who *pene* almost *præcurritis mihi* outstrip me *studio* in zeal; *sed* but *ut* that *mea vox* my voice *quæ* which *debet* ought *esse* to be *princeps* first *in republica* in the state, *videretur* might seem *functa* to have discharged *officio consulari* the duty of consul.

X. 20. *Nunc* now, *patres conscripti* conscript fathers, *antequam* before *redeo* I return *ad sententiam* to the vote, *dicam* I will say *pau.i* a few words *de me* about myself. *Ego* I *video* see *me* that I *suscepisse* have taken upon me *tantam multitudinem* as great a multitude *inimicorum* of enemies *quanta* as *est* is *manus* the band *conjuratorum* of conspirators, *quam* which *videtis* you see *esse* to be *permagnam* very great; *sed* but *judico* I judge *eam* it *esse* to be *turpem* base *et infirmam* and weak, *contemptam* contemptible *et abjectam* and abject. *Quod si* but if *aliquando* at any time *manus ista* that band *concitata* roused *furore* by the madness *et scelere* and crime *alicujus* of any one *plus valuerit* shall be more pow-

96

erful quam than *vestra dignitas* your dignity *ac reipublicæ* and that of the republic, *tamen* yet, *patres conscripti* conscript fathers, *me nunquam pœnitebit* I shall never repent *meorum factorum* of my deeds *atque consiliorum* and counsels. *Etenim* for indeed *mors* death, *quam* which *illi* they *fortasse* perhaps *minitantur* threaten *mihi* to me, *parata est* is in store *omnibus* for all: *nemo* [but] no one *assequutus est* has attained to *tantam laudem* such great praise *vitæ* in life *quanta* [as that] with which *vos* you *honorastis* have honoured *me* me *vestris decretis* by your decrees. *Semper enim decrevistis* for you have always decreed *cæteris* to the others *gratulationem* the congratulation *reipublicæ* of the state *bene gestæ* well administered, *mihi* but to me *uni* alone *conservatæ* [of the state] saved from ruin. 21. *Sit ille Scipio* be that Scipio *clarus* illustrious, *cujus consilio* by whose wisdom *atque virtute* and valour *Hannibal* Hannibal *coactus est* was compelled *redire* to return *in Africam* into Africa *atque* and *decedere* to depart *ex Italia* out of Italy; *alter Africanus* let the other Africanus *ornetur* be adorned *eximia laude* with distinguished praise, *qui* who *delevit* destroyed *duas urbes* two cities *infestissimas* most hostile *huic imperio* to this empire, *Carthaginem* Carthage *Numantiamque* and Numantia: *ille Lucius Paulus* let that Lucius Paulus *habeatur* be esteemed *vir egregius* an illustrious man, *cujus currum* whose [triumphal] chariot *potentissimus* that most powerful *et* and *nobilissimus rex* most noble king *Perses* Perses *quondam* formerly *honestavit* graced: *Marius* let Marius *sit* be *in eterna gloria* in eternal glory, *qui* who *bis* twice *liberavit* freed *Italiam* Italy *obsidione* from siege *et metu* and the fear *servitutis* of slavery: *Pompeius* let Pompey *anteponatur* be preferred *omnibus* to all, *cujus res gestæ* whose exploits *atque virtutes* and virtues *continentur* are contained *iisdem regionibus* within the same regions *ac terminis* and

97

bounds *quibus* as *cursus* the course *solis* of the sun.
Erit there will be *profecto* no doubt *aliquid loci*
some room *nostræ gloriæ* for our glory *inter laudes*
among the praises *horum* of these men ; *nisi* unless
forte by chance *est* it is *majus* greater *palefacere* to
lay open *nobis* to us *provincias* provinces, *quo*
whither *possimus* we may *exire* go forth, *quam* than
curare to provide *ut* that *etiam illi* those also *qui* who
absunt are away *habeant* may have [a place] *quo*
whither *revertantur* they may return *victores* con-
querors. 22. *Quanquam* although *conditio* the lot
externæ victoriæ of foreign victory *est* is *uno loco* in
one point *melior* better *quam* than *domesticæ* [that]
of a domestic one, *quod* that *hostes* enemies *alieni-
genæ* of foreign race *aut* either *serviunt* of slaves
oppressi when subdued *aut* or *recepti* received among
us *putant* think *se* that they *obligatos* are bound
beneficio by a benefit : *qui autem* but those who *ex
numero* out of the number *civium* of citizens, *depra-
vati* having been depraved *dementia aliqua* by any
madness, *cœperunt* have begun *semel* once *esse* to be
hostes enemies *patriæ* of their country, *quum* when
repuleris you have repelled *eos* them *a pernicie* from
[compassing] the ruin *reipublicæ* of the republic,
possis you may be able *nec* neither *coercere* to re-
strain them *vi* by force, *nec* nor *placare* to appease
them *beneficio* by kindness. *Quare* wherefore *video*
I see *æternum bellum* that eternal warfare *susceptum
esse* has been undertaken *mihi* for me *cum perditis
civibus* with [these] abandoned citizens ; *quod* which
ego confido I am confident *posse* may *propulsari* be
repelled *facile* easily *a me* from me *atque* and *a meis*
from mine *auxilio vestro* by your assistance *bono-
rumque omnium* and [that] of all good [men] *memo-
riaque* and the remembrance *tantorum periculorum* of
such great dangers *quæ* which *semper* always *hærebit*
will remain *non modo* not only *in hoc populo* among
this people *qui* which *servatus est* has been saved

sed etiam but also *in sermonibus* in the talk *ac* and
mentibus minds *omnium gentium* of all nations, *neque*
nor *vis ulla* will any force *reperietur* be found *tanta*
so great, *quæ* which *possit* may be able *perfringere*
to break through *et* and *labefactare* weaken *conjunctionem* the union *vestram* of you *equitumque
Romanorum* and the Roman knights, *et* and *tantam
conspirationem* so great unanimity *bonorum omnium*
of all good men.

XI. 23. *Quæ* which things *quum ita sint* being
thus, *conscripti patres* conscript fathers, *pro imperio*
instead of the command, *pro exercitu* instead of the
army, *pro provincia* instead of the province *quam*
which *neglexi* I have neglected; *pro triumpho* instead of a triumph, *ceterisque insignibus* and other
tokens *laudis* of honour, *quæ* which *propter custodiam* on account of the preservation *vestræ salutis* of
your safety *urbisque* and that of this city *repudiata
sunt* have been repudiated *a me* by me, *pro clientelis*
instead of the clientships *hospitiisque* and friend-
ship *provincialibus* in the provinces *quæ* which *tamen*
however *tueor* I support *non minore labore* with no
less labour *quam* than *comparo* I acquire them *urbanis opibus* through my influence in the city;
igitur therefore *pro his omnibus rebus* for all those
things *pro meis singularibus studiis* in return for my
conspicuous zeal *in vos* towards you, *proque hac
diligentia* and for that diligence *quam* which *con-
spicitis* you see *ad conservandam* to preserve *rempublicam* the state; *postulo* I require *nihil aliud*
nothing more *a vobis* from you, *nisi* except *memoriam*
the remembrance *hujus temporis* of this time *totiusque
mei consulatus* and of all my consulship. *Quæ* which
dum as long as *erit* it will be *infixa* fixed *vestris
mentibus* in your minds *arbitrabor* I shall think *me*
myself *septum esse* to be surrounded *firmissimo
muro* with a most firm wall. *Quod si* but if *vis* the
violence *improborum* of the factions *fefellerit*

99

have disappointed *atque* and *superaverit* triumphed over *meam spem* my hope *commendo* I recommend *vobis* to you *parvum meum filium* my little son, *cui* to whom *profecto* assuredly *erit* there will be *satis præsidii* sufficient aid *non solum* not only *ad salutem* for safety *verum etiam* but also *ad dignitatem* for dignity *si* if *memineritis* you shall bear in mind *illum* that he *esse* is *filium* the son *ejus* of that man *qui* who *conservaverit* preserved *suo solius periculo* at his own risk alone *hæc omnia* all these things. *Quapropter* wherefore, *patres conscripti* conscript fathers, *decernite* decide *diligenter* promptly *ac* and *fortiter* firmly *ut* as *instituistis* you have begun to do, *de summa salute vestra* about your general safety, *populique Romani* and that of the Roman people, *de conjugibus vestris* about your wives *ac* and *liberis* children, *de aris* about your hearths *ac* and *focis* homes, *de fanis* about your shrines *ac* and *templis* temples, *tectis* houses *ac* and *sedibus* dwellings *totius urbis* of the whole city, *de imperio* about your empire, *de libertate* about your liberty, *de salute* about the safety *Italiæ* of Italy, *deque universa republica* and about the whole republic. *Habetis enim* for you have *eum consulem* such a consul *qui* who *non dubitet* will not hesitate *parere* to obey *vestris decretis* your decrees, *et* and *quoad* as long as *vivet* he shall live *possit* will be able *defendere* to defend *et* and *præstare* to execute *per se ipsum* of himself *quæ* whatever thing *statueritis* you shall order.